In memory of our friend Sir George Henry Martin CBE

....

(1926 - 2016)

soundbreaking

Stories from the Cutting Edge of Recorded Music

....

Foreword by Sir George Martin

Edited by Sandra Choron

Introductory essays by Robert Santelli

Featuring portraits by Robert Essel

....

Published by

HIGHER
GROUND

BOOK PRODUCTION: MARCH TENTH, INC.
ART DIRECTION: SANDRA CHORON
INTERION DESIGN: HARRY CHORON
COVER DESIGN: ERIK DJANUISMADI
PROJECT MANAGER: BARBARA ZADINA

Higher Ground LLC
1818 N Street, NW
Suite 800
Washington, D.C. 20036

ISBN: 978-1-4951-7753-8

———

PRINTED IN CHINA, FIRST PRINTING, 2016

CONTENTS

FOREWORD

We humans have listened to music since the dawn of time. From simple rhythms hammered out by primitive man thousands of years ago to the sophisticated and intricate symphonic compositions of the nineteenth and twentieth centuries, we have all enjoyed music and the emotions it brings.

Around the world today more recorded music is heard than ever before. It is a truly global language. It helps us to communicate, it makes us happy, it can make us sad. It has helped to shape society as we know it today.

I have been fortunate enough to work in the recording business for most of my life. I have helped many talented songwriters and musicians to realize their ideas and to record their work for the world to hear. I have witnessed technological advances that have enabled us to develop recording so that it has become within the reach of everyone. History may prove me wrong, but I suspect that in many years to come people will look back and listen to the recordings of the late twentieth and early twenty-first centuries and reflect on this era as the golden age of a new art form.

This book helps to celebrate the work of some of the people behind the recordings; people who have excelled in their passion to record great music. In doing so, they have made all our lives that little bit richer.

George Martin

PREFACE

M usic has been part of human existence from the very beginning. Recorded music is something we take for granted today, but it has actually been with us for just over one hundred years. Beginning in the late nineteenth century with the experiments of Thomas Edison and Alexander Graham Bell with tin foil and wax cylinders, and Emile Berliner's breakthrough with the gramophone, sound recording has inspired musical innovation and has never ceased to evolve in both form and content. Technological advancements—including the use of microphones and amplification, magnetic tape, multitracking, and digital technologies—have influenced the music created, allowed artists to reach an increasingly larger audience, and made a profound impact on society. Today, computer technologies have matured to the point where anyone can record music and reach an audience of millions—all from their living rooms. The history of recorded music is one of the most important stories of the twentieth century. It is a story that needs to be told.

This book is part of the *Soundbreaking* initiative—an examination of the history of recorded music. The *Soundbreaking* eight-hour documentary film series examines the interplay of technological and musical innovations; presents the stories of some of the greatest artists of our time—what influenced them, and how they influenced others; and observes the impact that recorded music has had on society and our culture. This book focuses on the comments of a number of remarkable artists whose work has touched and been touched by the evolution of recorded music.

The *Soundbreaking* project grew out of a relationship between Sir George Martin and the Langstaff family—a relationship that dates back to the 1950s when Sir George produced recordings in England for the young American baritone John Langstaff. Sir George went on to become the legendary producer of the Beatles and many other artists over a career that spanned more than six decades. During that time, he witnessed the evolution of recording technologies, pioneering many of them, and saw the increasing interplay between recorded music and changing societal cultures and norms.

Sir George Martin is the inspiration and intellectual force behind the *Soundbreaking* project. The fact that over two hundred extraordinary singers, songwriters, producers, and other artists have come together to tell this story is a testament to the respect and love they hold for Sir George, and the widespread recognition of his role and impact on the history and evolution of recorded music.

As Sir George said, "Music is the soundtrack of our lives." As such, music touches all of us – it makes us better people, and the world a better place. Thank you, George...

David H. Langstaff
Higher Ground

ACKNOWLEDGMENTS

Higher Ground extends our gratitude to the following people whose support and assistance helped to make the *Soundbreaking* book and series possible:

James V. Baird and family, Glenn V. Kinsey and family, Mr. and Mrs. Norman V. Kinsey, Christopher M. Kinsey, Rebecca L. Kinsey, Richard N. Kinsey, and the Langstaff family.

Adam Sharp, Barbara Zadina, James Guerra, Joel Schoenfeld, Eric Schwartz, Alexandra Jiga, Lloyd Brown, Lawrence Russo, Robert Santelli, Jennifer Peel, Samuel Brylawski, George Massenburg, Alan Benson, Robert Essel, Karen Thompson, Dan Hamby, Tina Waganer, Nancy Sullivan, and Dave Paro.

Michael A. Bell, Lauren Browning, Bob and Marcie Zlotnik, George and Ann Colony, Edward J. Crawford III, Katherine C. Weir, John Atkins Crawford, Alison Atkins Crowther, Susanna Atkins McCarthy, William J. Atkins Jr., John E. Atkins, Edward J. Crawford IV, Robert W. Crawford, Andrew A. Crawford, John Henry Crawford, Donald W. Weir III, Caroline Weir Dixon, Juliette Louise Crowther and William John McCarthy, Dr. John C. Hardin III and Sally H. Hardin, Ann Kennedy and Geoffrey Walker, Andrew D. Klingenstein, David H. Langstaff, Ian McElroy, Tem and Maggie McElroy, William L. Ritchie Jr., Mark and Maritza Ross, Sanjay Shah, Jacquelyn and William Sheehan, and Thomas P. Steindler.

Joseph P. Allen, Mac and Susan Dunwoody, Nathaniel W. Foote, John and Linda Fuchs, George Hornig, Mary and Jim Kozlowski, Lynn Amato Madonna, Mark Thomas, and William Young.

Maro Chermayeff, Jeff Dupre, Josh Bennett, Julie Shapiro Thorman and the team at Show of Force Productions.

Principal interviews conducted, directed and produced by Joshua Bennett, Jeff Dupre, Maxim Langstaff, Julia Marchesi, George Martin, and Warren Zanes.

The GRAMMY Foundation, the GRAMMY Museum, and the Rock and Roll Forever Foundation.

Beth Hoppe, Bill Gardner, Mike Kelley, Jack Dougherty, Shawn Halford, Carrie Johnson, Jennifer Ruppman, Erin O'Flaherty and our friends at the Public Broadcasting Service (PBS), Hayley Dickson, Reece Scelfo and the team at Fremantle Media International, Christine LeGoff, Marie Drogue and her team at Ma Drogue A Moi (MDAM), and Mark Stevens, Shannon Cooper, Alexis Logan Wixted, and the team at RLJ Entertainment, Inc.

Mitchell Silberberg and Knupp LLP for legal and business affairs advice, Van Wagner Sports and Entertainment for sponsor marketing services, PMK. BNC for brand strategy and marketing services, Arcade Creative Group (a Sony Music Company) for title name and logo development, and Sandra and Harry Choron at March Tenth for book development.

Christopher Langstaff for his assistance to photographer Robert Essel. Original concept created by Maxim Langstaff for Wildheart Entertainment.

With our deepest gratitude to Lady Judy Martin, Giles Martin and the Martin family, and in loving memory of our friend Sir George Martin CBE.

soundbreaking

Stories from the Cutting Edge of Recorded Music

❖ george martin ❖

In the early 1960s, George Martin took the music of four lads from Liverpool and shaped it and sharpened it. In doing so, he helped change the course of popular music and, in the process, all of us. The Beatles and Sir George Martin made for a memorable team at Abbey Road Studios in London all those years ago. Even so, it would have been impossible to predict the incredible, world-changing success they'd enjoy together.

The Beatles—John Lennon, Paul McCartney, George Harrison, and Ringo Starr—were a rock and roll band, seasoned, sure, and pretty much unbeatable in England in the early sixties. But their original material lacked focus then and they were novices in the recording studio. Martin, on the other hand, was classically trained and had produced mostly comedy and novelty acts for EMI Records in the fifties. His experience and interest in pop music, particularly rock and roll, was limited and when he first heard the Beatles on tape (the band had auditioned earlier for Decca Records in London and was not offered a recording contract), he was not overly impressed.

But to Martin's credit, he did not entirely dismiss the band and offered the Beatles a record deal in mid-1962, citing the wonderful way the vocals of McCartney and Lennon worked together and the overall wit of the band, which seeped through, whether called for or not.

The Beatles' story, of course, is well documented. Now, more than fifty years after Martin first met the band, there have been hundreds of books, thousands of magazine sto-ries, and millions of words written about the band. Martin himself has spoken about the Beatles and his relationship with them countless times, and few cultural and music historians have underestimated his importance to the success of the Beatles. Martin, in fact, was often called "the Fifth Beatle."

Listening to the studio work of Sir George Martin and the Beatles, from their first single, "Love Me Do," released in 1962, through "I Want to Hold Your Hand," "I Saw Her Standing There," "Eleanor Rigby," and "Nowhere Man," through the albums *Rubber Soul* and *Revolver, Sgt. Pepper's Lonely Hearts Club Band, Abbey Road,* and *The White Album,* it's remarkably easy to see and, most importantly, hear, the sound of absolute genius at work.

So much of rock and roll is of the moment. The best songs and the best artists hit you hard and heavy in the present, the now. The music of the Beatles, with the masterly production guise of Sir George Martin, hit us all back then both beautifully and forcefully. But here's the thing: it hasn't lost any of its punch, not one bit, more than a half century later.

Martin made sure of that. His studio wisdom and musical ability matched with a keen understanding that he was working with extraordinary talent—something he knew he had a deep responsibility to—made the music work; made it mean special things to the world. And it made the world a better place.

ON LOVING MUSIC

Music has the ability to transcend races throughout the world. It is the universal language. I can go to Italy and not speak Italian and still be able to conduct an orchestra. Even without speaking any language, we can communicate by music itself. It is a binding influence for human beings. And wherever they go, there is music. And wherever there is music, they join together.

A beautiful piece of music, heard for the first time, can have a strong effect; it's a bit like falling in love. As a child, I listened to a piece by Debussy, "L'après-mi-di d'un faune," and I couldn't believe that these gorgeous sounds were being made by ordinary human beings blowing into bits of reed and scraping cat gut over strings. It was an amazing thing.

And I fell in love with music.

ON HOW RECORDED MUSIC CHANGED THE WORLD

It's almost impossible for a young person of today to imagine what the world could have been like without music on recordings, because the only way you could hear music a hundred years ago was by listening to someone playing it live.

It wasn't until a monk in the eleventh century hit upon the idea of notating musical notes that music started becoming accessible and fixed. Before that time, being passed down from one generation to another, music constantly mutated. Once we were able to fix it by means of notation, we could actually hear what was intended by the writer. And that was the great beginning of our golden era in music. From then on, everything has been written down. But more than that, in the last hundred years, everything has been recorded as well, so we can actually hear the sounds that were created. And that's a tremendous gift.

Before recordings, the average person in most countries never really got to hear anything but local folk music, maybe an accordion, violin, singing, whatever. Certainly in Victorian times, people used to make their own music by gathering around a piano as part of their social lives. The privileged, of course, could go to concerts in the main cities, but the vast majority of people, the peasants in America, the peasants of Britain and Europe, never had that opportunity.

Once recorded sound was invented, it changed the world. You could hear music from another country, in all kinds of com-binations. Communications and transport were very difficult in those days and so the chance of hearing a Beethoven symphony for someone in the wilds of Omaha was really impossible. The record changed that. Now they could listen to a Beethoven symphony on records in their homes, and it brought music right into the heart of the family.

It all started with Thomas Edison's dream. The dream was to record and play back sound. Edison was an engineer who realized that sound vibrations could be translated into physical movement. No one had actually done that before. And of course, there was no electricity at that time.

He knew that a diaphragm vibrated according to the sounds in the air, and he reasoned that if he could attach a stylus to that diaphragm, it could carve a track in something soft.

Thomas Edison with his phonograph, 1879

His first machine was a drum on which he would place the "something soft," which in this case was a piece of tin foil that he would wrap around the drum. The stylus would be placed up against it, and by rotating the drum, that stylus would cut the sounds into the tin foil. To play back, all you had to do was remove the stylus from one side, turn the machine around, and put another stylus, attached to a play-back diaphragm, on the other side, and rotate again.

It was really a very crude machine and it had many disadvantages because the tin foil was only capable of being played once or twice, and it couldn't handle music at all. But in 1877, it was a marvel, a miracle—it had never been done before. This was the first time that man had ever heard recorded sound.

But Edison had a rival, Alexander Graham Bell, the inventor of the telephone, and it was Bell who had the idea of using a wax cylinder for recording, an idea that Edison took up and used in his machine called a phonograph. No longer did you have to crank it by hand—it was now driven by clockwork so it was very much more steady than the old one. Most importantly, you could record music on it. And it could be played back time and again.

Then in 1888 a German immigrant to the United States, Emile Berliner, made the quantum leap in recorded sound. His invention—the gramophone, he called it—actually used a flat disk instead of a cylinder.

The great thing about this was that the disk could be pressed out in thousands, like biscuits. Mass production had come to music.

There were many advantages to these machines. One of them was that the machine was fairly portable. It didn't require electricity; you just wound it up. And you could take this little suitcase with you wherever you went and play your favorite records.

You couldn't make your own records on this machine, but it did bring great artists into thousands of homes, and thus the modern music industry was established by the gramophone. It was the first mass medium of the twentieth century.

When Edison invented recorded sound, music became immortal.

ON THE ELECTRIC GUITAR

In the early days of innocence, before rock and roll came along and swamped us with its sounds, the electric guitar really was not a significant instrument. Bands used to use guitarists, but the amplifiers they had were very small, and the frequency range and the volume of them was rather dire.

But that was what the musicians of the day wanted. They didn't want those guitars to sound too raucous. They just wanted them for rhythm. Once the principle of the electric guitar was established, there were a number of people who started making them. Les Paul and Leo Fender, in the United States, started thinking about guitars and how they could be improved. They designed different forms of induction that were seated in the body of the guitar. The strings were made a little bit heavier. They invented a lever that could actually vary the length of a note and sort of put a "bend" on it.

With these innovations, the guitar became something new. It became the weapon

"Rock and rollers wanted something that was going to assail the ears, and the electric guitar was the most convenient way of doing that."

of the rock and roll brigade, and the sounds that it could make were limited only by the power of the amplifier that was delivering them. Rock and rollers wanted something that was going to assail the ears, and the guitar was the most convenient way of doing that. The Fender Stratocaster became the model for all time. It still is revered among rock and roll artists, even though it was developed more than fifty years ago.

It wasn't just the loudness of the electric guitar that was so appealing. It's a very versatile instrument that can do an enormous number of things. It can play chords, it can play lines, and those lines can be bent, and you can get a bluesy kind of feeling out of it. The new sound was more raucous than ever before: rock and roll was born.

ON THE INVENTION OF THE MICROPHONE

Just as the electric guitar opened the doors to an entire genre of music, the microphone changed the way that people could use one of the most important instruments of all: the human voice. Suddenly it wasn't necessary to sing at maximum volume; you could get near the microphone and almost whisper into it, and it would come out as a whisper. But of course you had to develop a good technique.

Of all the great singers of the time, the most successful of that period was probably Bing Crosby, the first crooner. He developed a most wonderful technique of using the microphone. If he wanted to increase his volume, he tended to move back a little bit, and on a really quiet bit he would move in. It was the beginning of the

art of microphone technique.

The microphone also enabled the untrained singer to reach a new level of performance, while its subtlety gave an immediacy to what a performer was doing, and he could think more about the words. If he was singing a love song, he could sing with a certain intimacy instead of belting out the song in a hall before an audience that was eighty yards away. It also enabled the performer to sing quietly against a very loud accompaniment, and that was very necessary, given the music that was to come.

ON MULTITRACK RECORDING

Les Paul was an innovator, and he was one of the first people to design a multitrack recording machine. Multitrack did many things for us. It meant we could create sounds that couldn't be accomplished in a live performance, and it encouraged artists to think ahead, about layering one sound on top of another.

The effect of this multitrack was that you could do one thing and then put something on top of it—a layer cake principle. You could build your base, add a nice bit of jam, and then another bit of cake, and another bit, and so on, until you actually had a whole collection of sounds, which then had to be mixed. And you would then spend ages getting the mix right.

Soon the studio became a place where musicians could pool their resources and their talent into a melting pot that became multitrack recording.

ON THE RECORDING STUDIO

From those early days of Edison, with his

Bing Crosby, 1940

little bit of tin foil, we've now got to the point where music is infinitely accessible. Anybody in the world can listen to any piece of music at any time, in any place. And that has changed our lives. We can listen to improvised performances that would otherwise have been lost for all time—great pieces of music that might start as an idea in someone's head and then go on to be developed in a recording studio. Music could actually be created in the studio. The studio became a workshop.

The recording studio and its technology has changed music quite a bit. When I first came into the record business, the ideal for any recording engineer in a studio was to make the most lifelike sound he possibly could. He wanted to make music—a perfect copy of a photograph, so to speak—that was absolutely accurate, so that you couldn't tell it from the real thing.

The studio changed all that, because now, instead of taking a great photograph, we could start painting a picture. And we didn't have to be clinically accurate; we could create sounds that weren't possible in a concert hall.

There was a wonderful pianist named Glenn Gould who refused to play live, insisting that only on record could he get what he wanted, and that was his idea of perfection. I like a bit of humanity in my recording. I think music needs humanity; it needs soul. I don't mind if something is a little bit out of tune if it comes from a great artist with a great voice. But nowadays it's possible to tune a voice digitally. It's possible to correct things that are out of tempo. And people become obsessive with this, trying to make records that are perfect, in their eyes. I think the danger with this obsessive search

for perfection means that you can spend as long as you like in the studio. Perfection is an elusive goal, and a dangerous one to pursue.

I remember saying to John Lennon that I thought we did pretty well with all the stuff we recorded together, and he said, "I'd like to record it all again."

And I said, "What? Everything?" And he said, "Yeah." I said, "What about 'Strawberry Fields Forever?' And he looked at me and he lowered his glasses and he said, 'Especially *Strawberry Fields.*'"

ON WORKING WITH THE BEATLES

When I first met the Beatles, I didn't think they were capable of writing a great hit song. The stuff that they'd shown me already in their demos wasn't particularly marvelous—songs like "One After 909" or "P.S. I Love You." "Love Me Do" was the best, and we made that our first record.

But there was no sign of the greatness that was to come. I thought, I've got a hit group here if I can find the right song. I knew that the sound they were making was right. I knew that the way they sang their combined harmonies was so effective that it could invade America—if we had the right song.

I had listened to their early versions of "Please Please Me," which was a dirge. It was an attempt at a Roy Orbison song— very slow and very mournful—and I said to them, "That's much too slow. If you double the speed and maybe add a bit of harmonica, we might get somewhere. Think about it."

They did think about it and they came back with the harmonica added, a nice up-tempo feel to it, and I was delighted.

In fact, when we finished the record, I pressed the intercom to the boys down in the studio and said, "Gentlemen, you have your first number-one song." That was a bit arrogant, but it was true.

When I signed the Beatles, I had a gut feeling about them, and I think it was their charisma that impressed me enormously. There were these four young men, rather cheeky, slightly arrogant—in fact, very sure of themselves. Most of all, they had charm. And I thought, well if I like them so much personally, that feeling's bound to come over with an audience. And if the audience feels the same way about them as I do, then they're already ahead, whatever the song is. So I knew that if I had a hit song, I would have a hit with the group.

After "Please Please Me," I said to the boys, "Okay, you've done a great job—you've written a great song. Can you do it again? Give me another song that's just as good as that."

They came back with "From Me To You," which was wonderful. And it was a hit.

And I said the same thing again. "Go and do another one." It was like a goose laying golden eggs—only I didn't think it would last. But it did. Their inspiration was their success, and their success was their inspiration. Their talent seemed to grow like a flower in a hothouse. It was sprung up from nowhere. Every song that they gave me was a gem, but most significantly, they hadn't copied what they'd done before. They were giving me a new song with a new thought each time, and I cherished them for that. It seemed unending, the material they gave me.

As the songwriting genius of the Beatles developed, from the simple pop song of their early days into the more sophisticated stuff that came later, their inquisitiveness, their curiosity, was always at the fore.

One of my jobs by this time was getting inside their minds to find out what they wanted. Whoever was the writer, whether it was John or Paul, or even George—I had to try and find out what they were trying to achieve.

With Paul it was easier than with most because he seemed to be the most traditional of the musicians. He wanted to explore orchestras. When I suggested he use strings, he immediately hit upon that way of doing it, or he would come to me and say, in the case of "Penny Lane," "I've heard this piccolo on a Bach piece. Can we use it?" Those ideas spurred him on in many ways.

John was much more tricky. John was not as articulate in what he wanted as Paul was. Quite often I would say to him, "What do you want to do with this?" and he would give me a kind of simile or a metaphor and would start talking in colors or in feelings, and I would have to try and interpret that into instruments and the basic things that you did in the studio.

The Beatles at work in 1966

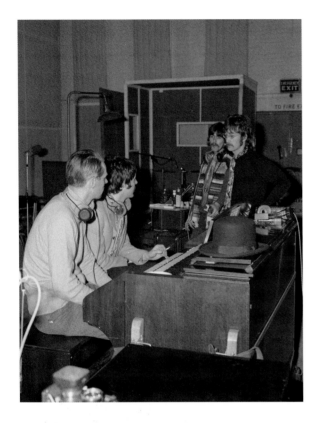

The Beatles, 1966

"I think music needs humanity; it needs soul. I don't mind if something is a little bit out of tune if it comes from a great artist with a great voice."

In the case of "Being For the Benefit of Mr. Kite," it was pretty obvious that he wanted a circus sound. But how to get it was another matter. John summed it up by saying, "Look, George, I want to smell the sawdust." And that was his way of telling me what we had to achieve.

The Beatles achieved a quantum leap when they stopped touring. They shocked their manager, Brian Epstein, to the core by saying, "We've had enough of this—living in this goldfish bowl, travelling from one hotel to another, concert after concert, television show after television show. We want to just work in the recording studio and produce our music there."

This was at the end of 1966, and the move gave us an opportunity that we hadn't had before. We no longer were under pressure to complete a song within a day or two days between their touring and appearances. We could spend as much time in the studio as we liked on it. And it gave the Beatles time to think and time to develop their creativity, in the studio. It led to a new era. We were experimenting with songs, we were thinking of ways of doing things differently.

When I first met them, the Beatles knew nothing about the recording studio. They had to learn about microphones and placements and relate loudness and so on. But they were very quick learners in the same way that their songwriting capabilities blossomed. So their appreciation of what went on in the studio blossomed, too.

Once we had time together, the studio became a workshop. George was the most technical of all. Paul was probably the most musical. John was aware of everything, but he let other people tend to studio considerations while he focused on the songs. And Ringo was just a great solid drummer. But he had great ideas too, and the others listened to him. If John played something and asked Ringo what he thought and Ringo said, "That's crap, John," he would immediately drop it. He wouldn't think about it twice. Ringo's opinion counted.

I well remember the night, in Paris, when I was awoken by a phone call from Brian Epstein, who was in a hotel around the corner, and he said, "Forgive me for waking you, George, but I knew you would want to hear this. We are number one in America!"

And of course I got out of bed and went 'round and we had a party. That was the most momentous thing ever, because it meant that we'd broken through the defenses, breached the walls, and from then on, America was the target and the place where the Beatles succeeded most of all. Other artists followed in the wake of the Beatles and became successful in America. And, for the first time in American history, the charts were not dominated by American acts—they were invaded by British acts. That didn't last forever—today there are very few British

acts in the American charts—but for a while, we were victors.

○ ○ ○

How many times have you heard a piece of recorded music which has transported you back to an event in your life that you remember vividly? It's most evocative, music, and it's a wonderful way of going back in time. In fact, music is the soundtrack of our lives.

❧ les paul ❧

Aside from being a major recording artist and performer in the 1950s, and a high-caliber guitarist who did things with six strings that made other players shake their heads in near disbelief, Les Paul, for all intents and purposes, gave us the solid-body electric guitar.

The arrival of the solid-body electric guitar in the early 1950s changed pretty much everything about American popular music. No genre was immune to its impact. More volume, more tones and textures, a fuller sound—they all came from the new instrument now being played by pop music's best guitar players. Les Paul's experiments with amplification years earlier and his dogged determination to get Gibson to pay attention to them finally came to fruition when the guitar company created the Les Paul model in 1952.

The Gibson Les Paul—now one of the most revered electric guitars in history—didn't start out with a bang. In fact, it was a bust. Gibson brought on Les Paul, not because they loved his ideas about amplification and solid-body guitars, but because its chief rival, Leo Fender and his Fender company, had released a successful mass-produced solid-body, first called the Squire, then the Broadcaster, and finally the name it goes by today, the Telecaster.

Fender's solid-bodies were simple and straightforward and sounded great. Gibson's Les Paul model had a garish golden finish, and the guitar promptly acquired the nickname "Gold Top." The look of the guitar and the lack of efficient marketing had a lot to do with the Les Paul model's less-than-impressive entry into the electric guitar market in the early 1950s. Gibson actually discontinued the Les Paul in 1960; Eric Clapton, Duane Allman, and other guitar gods of the late sixties salvaged its reputation.

Gibson wisely resumed the production of Les Paul models, and the rest, as they say, is history. The new model, along with the Fender Telecaster and the Stratocaster (the solid-body that followed the Telecaster in the Fender factory) comprise the blessed trinity of solid-body electric guitars in American popular music.

Through it all, Les Paul, the musician, managed to maintain a career that ultimately gained him entrance into the Inventor's Hall of Fame and the Rock and Roll Hall of Fame, among other honors. The career he had in the early fifties with his wife, Mary Ford, withered with the advent of rock and roll. But Paul's reputation as an innovative guitar stylist remained intact.

Playing a big part in the evolution of the solid-body electric guitar and making all those wonderful recordings with Mary Ford would have been enough to assure Les Paul a place in pop music history. But he didn't stop there. Add to his list of accomplishments the creation of overdubbing and multitracking in the recording studio. Those developments were nothing short of revolutionary when it came to making records.

Overdubbing, or the ability to add to a previously recorded piece of music, and multitracking, which meant that in the recording studio, drums could be put on one track, vocals on another, lead guitar on another, and so on, made music sound so much better and broadened the tools of the recording engineer in a way that redefined the job.

Les Paul changed the way musicians played music, the way engineers recorded music, and the way fans heard music. A genius? Absolutely. An essential part of the American music story in the years after World War II? Without a doubt.

ON LEARNING MUSIC BEFORE RECORDS BECAME AVAILABLE

When I got my first guitar from Sears and Roebuck, I heard that Gene Autry was going to appear in the town where I lived. I got my friend to get a flashlight and we sat right down there on the front row, and every few minutes I would say, "Now—hit the light." And he'd hit the light and I'd put a dot there on my guitar where Gene would put his finger.

This went on for maybe two days. And finally, Gene Autry announced, "There's something bothering me. Every time I hit this chord, a light goes on in the audience. What in the world is going on?"

So my friend said, "Hey, he's talking about you." And the next thing you know, I'm up on the stage and Gene shows me the chord. Then he hands me his guitar and he has me playing the chord.

That's what it was like back then: if you wanted to learn something, you'd have to go see someone in person and hear it. Today, you can just go out and buy the record and put it on. The world progresses and we're fortunate for it. That's why a young kid, maybe eight years old, can come on the stage today and play so much more than we could play when we were eight years old. Because he's exposed to all these tools that we are privileged to learn from.

ON HIS FIRST TV BROADCAST

Some time in the 1930s I had the privilege of watching President Roosevelt announce that there was a new media that was going to be given to the public and it was called television. That's how we heard about it for the first time. And you could see and hear the entertainer.

Soon enough, me and my band were booked for an hour on a Wednesday night to do a sound test. So we go up to RCA in New York City and I'll be darned if we're not the first ones to do a broadcast with an orchestra, as a sound test. So here we are, we're the first broadcast and the lights are so hot and the cameras are so large and we're stumbling over each other because this is all new to us.

Walter Winchell and Fred Allen were downstairs in a drugstore. After the show, we ran down there to see how we looked and they said we looked great. Well, we're now waiting for the mail to come in and we only received one letter from a guy in Parsippany, New Jersey, saying that he caught the show and he enjoyed it. So as far as I know, we had one listener on the first broadcast that we did.

ON THE TROUBLE WITH MULTITRACKING

I never saw Bing Crosby rehearse a day in my life. He walked into the studio and he just walked up and he wouldn't say anything to anybody. I'd give a downbeat and he'd just start to sing.

Bing had this great ability to learn something fast. His philosophy was, "Let them know I'm human." And so if he sang a song and there was a mistake, he left the mistake in.

On the other hand, Frank Sinatra may come along and say, "Well, I've only done this seventeen times; let's go for two more and I'll get it just the way I want it." And while one is perfect, the other one has so much of the kind of feeling to it that you get by doing something just one time. Being in the recording industry all my life, I've

"[Bing Crosby's] philosophy was, 'Let them know I'm human.' And so if he sang a song and there was a mistake, he left the mistake in."

Les Paul and Mary Ford pose for a 1955 advertisement.

seen it happen over and over, where a fellow will come in and record in my studio, and he would record something nineteen times. And then he plays them back and the guy decides that the best record of the bunch is the first one he did.

It has the most feeling, the most originality about it. It had a newness to it, it had all the things you don't have when you have the advantage of going back and saying, "Well, I'll fill that in later, I'll change it later." One of the biggest drawbacks in multitracking is the fact that we have the ability to fix it later. As you perfect the notes, you sacrifice so much in the feeling of that song. I've seen this happen many a time, and I've said, "Just leave it alone, don't change it. Just leave it the way it is."

ON LOUIS ARMSTRONG

The first time I worked with Eddie South, the great violinist, was in 1929. Eddie asked me if I would play guitar with him. We were going to do this at the Regal Theatre in Chicago.

When we got there, the act that was on ahead of us was this fellow playing the trumpet, and he missed the last note. So he says, "Well, I'll do it again." And so the audience is tensing up a little bit. And he goes back and he misses it again. He missed it three times. And I'm at the stage door entrance asking the stagehand there who that guy was playing the trumpet.

And he says, "I don't know; go look at the marquee." So I went out and looked at the marquee and I came back in and I said, "It's Louis Armstrong. My goodness, I'm working with Louis Armstrong!"

And I saw that he had missed those notes deliberately. He missed the note the first time. He missed the note the second time. The third time, he almost had it.

Now the people are sitting on the edges of their chairs, because they're all excited and they're rooting for this guy. He's going to hit it! And Louis hit that note and just tore the house down.

Louis Armstrong was one of the greatest showmen ever. I don't know of anybody that plays the trumpet that doesn't put Louis first.

ON THE BLUES

All our good music came from Afro-Americans and the blues. I'm not a blues player but the real good dirty blues that I liked to hear was a guy on the back porch with his guitar, where he doesn't know what chord he's playing, could care less about it. He has a message to deliver. And he delivers that message in his crying voice. Four bar—four beats to the bar—means nothing to him. He may put five in it, might be three. It's unimportant. He was just playing the blues.

ON THE BEST
GUITAR PLAYER EVER

I was with Walt Maguire from London Records one day about ten years after I had retired from the business, and I says to him,

"Find me all the great guitar players that are happening now. I'd like to hear what's happening in the music business today."

So they brought over a big stack of records. And I says, "Don't tell me the names of any of the guitar players, just play them for me and I'll listen to them. And I listened to all of them and just had them write down which ones I liked. Then I asked them to tell me who I picked as the best guitar player. Hands down, it was Eric Clapton. He was the guitar player that I enjoyed listening to the most, every time.

ON THE CAPITOL
RECORDS BUILDING

Glenn Wallichs from Capitol Studios came out to California and showed me the drawings of the round building. And I says, "Yeah, but where are you going to put the broom?"

The Capitol Records building, Los Angeles

❧ pete seeger ❧

If ever there was an ambassador for American folk music, it was Pete Seeger. Incessantly passionate about people, songs, and the power of combining them, Seeger was a walking folk music jukebox, a collector of hundreds, perhaps thousands, of songs and the stories behind them, a tunesmith who believed that every song has a purpose, every lyric part of the greater story of life. He brought his banjo everywhere he went as if it were an extension of his long, lanky frame. And as he got older and the whiskers on his face grew more gray, he began to take on the trappings of the wizened song sage, the Great Curator of the American folk tradition that he most surely was.

He was born into a music family. His father was Charles Seeger, a noted musicologist, and his mother, Constance, played and taught violin. Both were affiliated with Julliard, the prestigious conservatory in New York. Pete fell for folk music early on and learned the rudiments of the banjo and guitar before enrolling at Harvard University. Higher education, however, wasn't in the cards for Seeger, as he sought out authentic folk music experiences, mostly down South, a region rich with folk songs and traditions.

In his early twenties, Seeger was fortunate to meet and work with Alan Lomax, the musicologist and collector of folk songs for the Library of Congress. Through Lomax, Seeger also met Woody Guthrie, whose love of folk music was as great as Seeger's. Unkempt and raggedy, Guthrie was the singing hobo from the heartland whose Okie roots were real and whose determination to make every song he wrote a strong, unwavering statement about America, and he deeply impressed young Seeger. Soon, Seeger was on the road with Guthrie, learning everything he could from him and sharing in unique experiences, singing union songs at union halls, and hopping freights and hitching rides across America.

The experiences radicalized Seeger. A folk group he had formed prior to America's entry into World War II, the Almanac Singers, later included Guthrie and espoused socialist themes as artists and intellectuals sought a way to improve the lives and conditions of common folk and workers in America. After serving in the army, Seeger married and settled in New York. He continued to use song as a means to better America, but the times had changed. A Cold War had replaced the hot one, and suddenly any talk or singing about socialism was considered seriously anti-American.

Seeger suffered for his political beliefs. Another of his groups, the Weavers, scored a major pop hit with their rendition of Lead Belly's "Good Night, Irene," but when it was revealed that Seeger and the rest of the group had ties to socialism and even communism before the war, the Weavers' promising future promptly dried up. Seeger was blacklisted by the House Un-American Activities Committee in the 1950s and then struggled to maintain a career.

But Pete Seeger was a survivor. During the folk revival in the early 1960s, he became folk's elder statesman. He sang for civil rights workers and students against the war in Vietnam. Through music he advocated for human rights for everyone and became one of the very first artists in America to campaign for clean water and other ecological issues. Along the way, he influenced everyone from Bob Dylan to Bruce Springsteen. Guthrie withstanding, no other folksinger had the impact on America—and beyond—that Seeger did.

Pete Seeger passed away in 2014 at the age of ninety-four. He left behind a staggering legacy, reams of songs, and a life to be admired. He was an American patriot who used music to describe the country he loved and to make it better, too.

ON THE PURPOSE OF MUSIC

Many people assume that music is just for entertainment, to help you forget your troubles. I often put it this way: some music helps you forget your troubles, some music helps you understand your troubles. And some music helps you do something about your troubles. The father of George Frideric Handel, the famous composer, three centuries ago, told his son, "You shouldn't waste your time in music. Music is just for entertainment." As we know, his son didn't listen to his father. He went ahead and composed some of the greatest music that Europe ever knew.

ON FOLK MUSIC

Louis Armstrong said, "All music is folk music." And what he meant by that is that folks is folks everywhere. The term *folk music* was invented in the nineteenth century, and it meant the music of the peasant class. I often say that the most prominent folk music in twentieth-century America was rock and roll.

About a hundred years ago, a man in Texas named John Lomax started writing down cowboy songs, and he put out a book. He collected songs, and thanks to him, we know "Home on the Range" and a whole batch of cowboy songs. Lomax said, "These are good songs; I want people to sing them."

In the 1920s, during the Depression, President Herbert Hoover said to Rudy Vallee, a very famous pop singer, "Mr. Vallee, if you can sing a song that will make the American people forget the Depression, I'll give you a medal." Back then, people didn't want protest songs. If protest songs got written, they were not played on the radio or sold in the record stores. But just about

that time, my father got very interested in American folk music, and he met Alan Lomax. Lomax was in charge of the archive of American folk songs in the Library of Congress, and he was full of youth and enthusiasm and confidence. And he did things that other people might not have done ever.

He called up the head of CBS, William Paley, and said, "Mr. Paley, you have a school on the air. I think you should devote one year of it to letting the American people know about American folk music. I'll have this young fellow, Seeger, sing the songs." So suddenly I was introduced to thousands—not hundreds but thousands—of songs, American songs, through Alan Lomax.

When I heard these old songs, I suddenly found I was learning about my own country in ways that I'd never learned in school. And I learned that this extraordinarily multicultural diverse country we call the United States of America is full of mixtures—songs that are half this and half that.

Alan Lomax really started off the folk song revival. He was very conscious of what he was trying to do and he wrote books and made recordings and he taught people. He told Burl Ives, "Burl, you've learned a lot of wonderful songs from your grandmother back in Indiana. You don't need to be an actor. Thousands of people would come to hear you sing folk songs." And that's exactly what Burl did for a while until he got big jobs out in Hollywood. Alan Lomax brought a great blues singer up from North Carolina, Josh White. And he showed that there were white people in the north who would really like to hear his blues. Eventually, he even toured Europe.

Alan Lomax and Pete Seeger with unidentified musician, 1959

"Some music helps you forget your troubles, some music helps you understand your troubles. And some music helps you do something about your troubles."

Alan kept on recording in the country and I think it was around 1947 when he was on a collecting trip in Mississippi and he came across a man, McKinley Morganfield was his name. Lomax recorded him and said, "You should be known nationally, not just locally." And I guess he probably wasn't the only man who told that to Muddy Waters.

I use the term *folk music* as little as possible. It means so many different things to different people. It's a little like beer. You put a glass of warm English stout in front of an American and he spits it out and says, "Give me some beer!" Like *folk music,* the word *beer* means quite different things to different people. And so I literally don't use the term unless I have to.

ON WOODY GUTHRIE

I was helping Alan Lomax down in Washington when we heard that there was going to be an evening of singing, folk music—whatever you wanted to call it—in a theater on Broadway. They'd gotten the use of the theater for a midnight benefit for California farm workers.

One of the singers was a man named Woody Guthrie. And on the stage that night, there were a lot of well-known singers: Burl Ives, Lead Belly, and Josh White, and the Golden Gate Quartet singing gospel songs. And then this kind of short fellow, he must have been about five-foot-six, comes out with a cowboy hat on and boots and he tells stories and then sings a song he'd written, then he tells another story and then sings another song.

Alan told him, "Woody, you must come to Washington; we've got a recording studio down there, and I want to record every song you've written and other ones that you know."

Later on, I would accompany Woody. I had a good ear and he let me tag along after him. I was seven years younger than he was and he once said to somebody, "That guy Seeger is the youngest man I ever knew."

I learned things from him that I never would have learned anywhere else. He showed me how to hitchhike, how to ride freight trains. And after that year, we criss-crossed the country.

He taught me how to turn a nickel into a quarter in a bar. He says, "Pete, put your banjo on your back and go and buy a nickel beer and sip it as slow as you can. Sooner or later, somebody will say, 'Kid, can you play that thing?' Don't be too eager. Say, 'Maybe, a little.' Keep on sipping your beer. Sooner or later, somebody will say, 'Kid, I've got a quarter for you if you pick us a tune.' Now you swing your banjo around and play your best song." And with that advice, I never went hungry all year.

Woody was a creative genius—there's no other term for it. He taught me that it wasn't impossible for me to write songs. I had tried to but I wasn't much good at it and I didn't think of myself as a songwriter. But he got me started at it. I look upon myself as a link in a chain.

Woody Guthrie's "This Land is Your Land" never played on the radio and it was never sold in any music store. But it got in the schools because a tiny little record company called Folkways Records had recorded it. Maybe they sold a thousand copies.

But some teachers in New York, where the company was, liked the song and found the kids liked it. And they started singing it in the East and pretty soon, a publisher put

I AM DONE WITH GREAT THINGS
AND BIG THINGS, GREAT INSTITUTIONS
AND BIG SUCCESS, AND I AM FOR
THOSE TINY INVISIBLE MOLECULAR
MORAL FORCES THAT WORK FROM
INDIVIDUAL TO INDIVIDUAL, CREEPING THROUGH
THE CRANNIES OF THE WORLD LIKE SO
MANY ROOTLETS, OR LIKE THE CAPILLARY OOZING
OF WATER, YET WHICH IF YOU GIVE THEM TIME
WILL REND THE HARDEST
MONUMENTS
OF MAN'S PRIDE.
WILLIAM JAMES

Detail of the exterior of Pete Seeger's home in Beacon, New York, with thoughts by William James

it in a school songbook.

That was the only place the song was ever printed. It was never on any sheet music anywhere. But twenty years later, everybody in America knew this song.

ON BOB DYLAN

Bob Dylan disappointed a lot of people when he started going electric. And I was angry at the time, not because he went electric but because the sound was so distorted, it was so loud that you couldn't understand a word. And I liked hearing the words he sang. He was singing "Maggie's Farm." It's a great song and the words are very good. But you couldn't understand any of it. I ran over to the person in charge of the sound and said, "Fix the sound so you can hear the words." And he shouted back, "No, this is the way they want it." And probably they

wanted purposely to make a clean break with the folk music crowd. I remember thinking, Damn, if I had an axe I'd cut the cable.

ON "TURN, TURN, TURN"

I once got a letter from one of my publishers saying, "Pete, can't you write another song like 'Good Night Irene?' I can't market these protest songs you keep writing."

I was a little angry. I told him, "You'd better get yourself another songwriter; this is the only kind of song I know how to write." And off the top of my head, I improvised the tune for some great words I'd run across in Ecclesiastes in the Bible. I think I rearranged them very slightly so they'd rhyme a little better. And half an hour later, I put this song on tape and sent it to him. And he got back to me a week

later and said, "Wonderful, just what I was looking for!" And he got it to the Byrds, this fantastic, wonderful rock group, and they made a new arrangement. They changed a few of my notes, but these days, if I want an audience to join in with me, I sing their version.

ON SHARING MUSIC

My nephew was once in charge of the Archives of Traditional Music at the University of Indiana. And he receives a tape recording from Australia. And it's bound in sealing wax. And the letter with it says, "Do not break this sealing wax. You must not listen to this tape, you must not let anyone else listen to this tape unless somebody from Australia comes with proof that they are members of such and such a tribe of aborigines. I recorded it for these aborigines only on the promise that I would not play it for anybody. And they said that nobody but them are ever supposed to hear this piece of music, but they thought that maybe their great grandchildren may wonder, Are they singing the song right or are they changing it in a way it should not be changed?" And they wanted to keep it safe until the right person came along and was allowed to break the seal and listen to it. It's still sitting in the archives at the University of Indiana—sealed.

❧ tony bennett ❧

Tony Bennett was born in New York and raised to sing. His family recognized his vocal gift and gave him the encouragement to take it beyond the Sunday gatherings at the homes of relatives. Soon, Bennett was a singing waiter, then a nightclub singer waiting for his break. It came in 1949 in Greenwich Village, New York. Bennett was sharing the stage with another emerging talent, Pearl Bailey. In the audience was entertainer Bob Hope. Impressed with what he heard, Hope invited Bennett to sing uptown with him at the Paramount, the place where a few years earlier, Frank Sinatra had made the girls scream and swoon with dreamy delight.

This was the swing era; if you were a singer, you had to swing. You also had to be able to bring the song close to you, to make it seem as if those lyrics and the feeling behind them were an extension of yourself. Bennett could do that. Few could do it better. It led to a recording contract with Columbia Records after an audition in 1950 with Mitch Miller, the famed producer and talent scout. Bennett wasted no time in getting to the top of the pop charts. The following year Bennett's "Because of You" shot straight to number one and stayed there for a remarkable thirty-two weeks.

Bennett practically took up residency on the pop charts in the early 1950s. He covered a Hank Williams classic, "Cold, Cold Heart," marking one of the very first times a country song sung by a pop singer scored high on the charts. "Rags to Riches" went to number one in 1953. In all, Bennett scored a remarkable two dozen Top Forty hits by the time the Beatles changed everything in 1964, including his signature single and first Grammy winner, "I Left My Heart in San Francisco."

But to call Tony Bennett merely a pop singer would not be telling his full story. Bennett was just as much a jazz singer as he was someone who could sell records to mainstream listeners. His album *Basie Swings, Bennett Sings* (1959) still ranks as one of Bennett's best recordings and is firm proof of his jazz grasp. In addition to Basie, Bennett worked with Bill Evans, Ray Charles, Dexter Gordon, George Benson, and other jazz stalwarts, and recorded a jazz classic in 1964, *When Lights Are Low,* a tribute to Nat King Cole. Later in his career, he'd honor his good friend Sinatra with *Perfectly Frank* (1992), which was good enough to win Bennett another Grammy.

Bennett would continue to record and perform in the 1970s and well beyond. He won more Grammys, received more awards, was named a Kennedy Center Honoree in 2005, and in 2006 was lauded by the National Endowment for the Arts as a Jazz Master. Tony Bennett has remained a steady presence in pop and jazz for nearly seventy years. In all those years, he simply sang, as he would say. Which is what he is still doing. Whether it's on his own or with Lady Gaga, Tony Bennett is simply still singing.

Tony Bennett, 1970

ON EARLY INFLUENCES

I grew up during the Depression. And it was very, very difficult. There was barely any food on the table. My mom was a seamstress, and she used to work on a dress for a penny to help feed three children. We were one stage away from complete poverty, and we couldn't buy a record that we liked, like it is today. When my father bought a record it had to be one that the whole family would like. And it was the best thing that ever happened to us.

He bought a record by Enrico Caruso on Victor Records. And that record pointed us to the rest of our lives—toward culture, toward quality. And ever since then, everything else was superfluous in my life. It was the best beginning of education as a child that you could ever get, listening to the great Caruso, the greatest singer that ever lived in opera.

Now, the reason that my father bought that record is that he had quite a reputation himself. He was an immigrant from Italy, from Calabria, the boot of Italy, and there's a legend in my family that my father would sing on the top of a mountain in Calabria and the whole valley would be able to hear him. He had a beautiful voice.

That record, together with the story about my father, changed my brother's life and mine. Listening to Caruso, my brother was smitten by how beautiful it was and decided to take lessons and became very popular at his age; he was only eleven or twelve years old, and they called him the "Little Caruso." He was on the radio in those days, and he sang in the Metropolitan Opera. I became envious of my brother because he was getting all the action.

To compete with him, I ended up being the entertainer while he was studying opera. Soon my whole family would come over and they would make a circle around my brother, my sister, and myself. And we would entertain the family. They would take out the guitars and the mandolins and we would entertain them every Sunday. We had a grand time.

ON MARKETING MUSIC

I think the great part of the beginning of the record business was that it taught everybody to choose the records they really liked. Gene Austin made a record—"Whippoorwills call, evenin' is nigh, hurry to my blue heaven." Everybody wanted that record. This was before Bing Crosby, and it became phenomenal. Everybody that heard the record on the radio wanted to buy this record, so they bought a Victrola to play it on. And what happened is, they created collectors.

The record stores encouraged the public to collect records, to have a library of their own of records that they liked. The big mistake is that the record industry walked away from that format. Soon you no longer collected records, you just bought whatever the advertisers insisted you have to buy. They manipulated the public instead of just leaving it up to them to go into a record shop, listen to some records, and then say, "This is the one I'd like."

So it's no longer a collector's profession. These days, records last maybe ten or twelve weeks and are forgotten. We're

losing something as a culture. Today there's an insistence that the public is not as intelligent as the marketing people. They look down at the public.

When Thomas Edison sent a phonograph machine to Arthur Sullivan [of Gilbert and Sullivan], Sullivan wrote back, "I'm terrified that . . . so much bad and hideous music will be put on record forever."

Well, Mr. Sullivan was very correct. You know, today there's a devaluation and disrespect for the public. I really resent that. I never look down at an audience. I look up to them. I'm a servant on that stage.

ON IRA GERSHWIN

It happened to me one day; it only happened once in my life: I met the great Ira Gershwin. This was at Chapel Music. He wanted me to do a song that was supposed to be in a Fred Astaire movie but they didn't put it in. It's a wonderful song, written by George and Ira Gershwin, called "High Hopes." A beautiful recording. So Ira said to the clerk at Chapel, "Get that music for Mr. Bennett; I'd like him to hear this record." The clerk was all excited about helping Ira Gershwin, and he came back and he said, "Mr. Gershwin, we not only have the music, but we have a record of it in stereo." And Ira Gershwin said, "I

don't need stereo, I have two ears!"

Now, the reason he said that is that he just wanted a good performance. He didn't care if it was stereo or quadraphonic or digital or whatever. He just wanted a good performance from an artist, to communicate the song and make the song work. And that taught me that a recording should really sound as close to a live performance as possible.

ON JAZZ AND RACISM

The first jazz record that ever came out was by a white jazz artist, because the record companies said that the black artists would never sell down South. This had been going on for a long time. What a tragedy, what a waste of great talent that the very fellas that invented improvised jazz were deprived of it. Jazz is one of the great art forms in the world, and it comes out of New Orleans, from a guy called Louis Armstrong. It's the most phenomenal music in the world. Jazz is my favorite music because it's spontaneous and it's in the moment. And it's honest and it's truthful and it's not pre-planned. It's right now, this is how you feel at that second. It's full of integrity, it's full of quality, it is not junk. It lasts forever.

Fats Waller wrote "Ain't Misbehavin'" on a brown paper bag during a jam session up in Harlem. They gave him two bottles of gin. That's what Fats Waller got paid for "Ain't Misbehavin'," which made millions and millions of dollars with the show on Broadway, and every record artist in the world, including myself, has recorded it. It's a great song that broke internationally and made millions of dollars. And Fats Waller got two bottles of gin for the song. Look at the sin of that.

ON SINGING

What makes a singer? It's a God-given gift. It's someone who spiritually gets the whole message of the love of singing, to love what you're doing. Where you *have* to do it. It's not that you *want* to do it; you *have* to do it. To this day, my teachers are the audience. Every night that I hit that stage, I walk off at the end of the performance learning something from what the audience reacted to. I learn what to leave out, what to put in. My teacher is an audience.

You have to understand that Bing Crosby created the art of intimate singing. That was the microphone. Before that, there was Ethel Merman and Al Jolson, and they had to hit the back of the house without a microphone. All of a sudden, the microphone

With Lady Gaga at Radio City Music Hall, New York, 2015

comes along and it was Bing who was smart enough to say, "Hey, I could whisper in this into someone's ear." Very intimate. But a microphone is really like a wall between the audience and yourself. It's mechanical. It's not a natural sound.

Now, when I perform, the biggest thing I do when I play an acoustical hall is put the microphone down and sing without it. And that's the thing everybody remembers.

"When Thomas Edison sent a phonograph machine to Arthur Sullivan [of Gilbert and Sullivan], Sullivan wrote back, 'I'm terrified that . . . so much bad and hideous music will be put on record.'"

❧ frankie valli ❧

He is a genuine Jersey boy. In fact, it's his story and the story of the group he sang with, the Four Seasons, which resonated so strongly on Broadway years ago—and continues to make people sing and cheer in the theater night after night. *Jersey Boys,* the musical, isn't just a Jersey story; it's an American story about getting to the top, of dreaming a dream and then overcoming the odds to make it real.

Frankie Valli had a near unpronounceable last name—Castelluccio—unpronounceable, that is, if you didn't grow up in the Italian-American neighborhoods of Newark or Belleville, New Jersey, where Italian kids would learn from the black kids how to sing, and the two would make great music called doo-wop. Frankie made it simple: Valli, so that there would be no forgetting it.

It was a good thing, because in the early sixties, the Four Seasons became regulars on the pop charts. They were hit makers and heartthrobs, and they were living the American Dream out loud. On the West Coast the Beach Boys brought to American pop their shiny, seamless, sunny harmonies about surf and sun and fun. On the East Coast, the Four Seasons had their harmonies too—plus Valli's striking falsetto. But their story and sound were tougher, more black, and Jersey cool.

The Four Seasons and the Beach Boys practically owned the radio airwaves in the early sixties. Pop music would be forever altered in 1964 with the arrival of the Beatles, but both American groups had staying power and endured the British onslaught, at least for a while. For Valli and the Four Seasons, the hits started with the easy shuffle of "Sherry," a number-one smash that introduced the Four Seasons' urban harmonies in full force. "Sherry" was all over the radio in late 1962, and it was just a hint of what was to come.

"Big Girls Don't Cry" and "Walk Like a Man" made for three number-one hits in less than a year, along with a slew of other eventual Top Ten hits, including "Candy Girl," "Dawn," "Let's Hang On," "Working My Way Back to You," "I've Got You Under My Skin," and "Tell It to the Rain." It was an impressive body of work. Through it all, Valli's falsetto fueled the hits. Having Bob Gaudio pen most of the songs for the Four Seasons while providing impeccable backup harmonies was a winning combination, good enough to buck the Beatles and make sure Jersey would stay on the music map until Bruce Springsteen made his presence known a decade later.

Pop music never stood still in the sixties; it moved fast, even furious, at times, and if an artist or a group didn't keep up, they were passed by. It happened to the Beach Boys, and it happened to the Four Seasons, too. By the late sixties the Four Seasons had fizzled. Valli turned solo in the early seventies, retiring for the most part the falsetto that made him and the Four Seasons famous. The Valli voice we now heard was more soulful, exhibited more range, and was better able to portray a wider range of emotion. The hits started again: "My Eyes Adored You," "Swearin' to God," and Valli's version of "Our Day Will Come." Then, out of nowhere, the Four Seasons roared back with a pair of pop gems: "Who Loves You" and "December 1963 (Oh What a Night)." It wouldn't last; Valli and his old group parted ways, again. But good music and good stories have a way of coming back, and theirs did just that. *Jersey Boys* broke theater records, and there, right in the middle of that irresistible tale was the sound of Frankie Valli and the Four Seasons, sounding as fresh as ever, like it had never left us.

Frankie Valli, 1960

ON GROWING UP WITH MUSIC

For me, music is the very life and soul and breadth of what I'm all about. I couldn't imagine my life without music. The first music I heard was the records that my father was playing of Enrico Caruso. I don't know if I took anything from Caruso, but it was quite amazing to me to hear a man sing and hit some of the notes that he was hitting. My father also played a lot of classical music. He also played Bing Crosby and, later, Perry Como. And the guy that was my favorite of all of those guys was Frank Sinatra. But the first records that I actually bought were jazz—probably Stan Kenton. I was really into jazz. Back then, there were people like Dinah Washington and Little Jimmy Scott and Ray Charles and all of the very early R&B

groups like the Ravens and the Orioles and the Harptones and the Clovers. Fortunately for me, I grew up at the tail end of the big band era, and I had a taste of all of it. I got to actually witness each band playing live. I never really wanted to become a pop singer. I was more interested in jazz, and later on, I really got into R&B.

ON EARLY RADIO

I wish that there was today as much radio as there was when I was growing up as a kid. I can remember just in the area of New York and New Jersey, there had to be at least fifteen or twenty radio stations playing music. In those days they played the Top Forty records, but they also played new songs by new artists. A pop station would play anything from R&B to Sinatra. Today

The Four Seasons, 1964. *From left*: Frankie Valli, Bob Gaudio, Nick Massi, Tommy DeVito.

they won't play a record unless it's a hit, so how does it become a hit?

ON FALSETTO SINGING

Part of the Four Seasons breakthrough was that we used falsetto differently than everybody else did. Everybody else used it as background. We used it as background, too, but then we began to sing leads in falsetto and that really was the key. We used it full force and that's what created the style of the Four Seasons. At the time, I thought everybody could sing that way. Since I never had any lessons, I figured everybody can do falsetto. I just took it for granted that everybody could do it. Then as time went on I realized that it was really a special gift. I began to realize the impact that we had on the industry when a lot of groups after us came along and used falsetto to try and copy us.

ON RECORD PROMOTION

Back in the day when you were breaking a record, there were certain cities you went to in order to promote the record—Detroit, Philadelphia, Baltimore. You'd go to that city and spend an entire day from seven in the morning until maybe ten, eleven at night, going to different radio stations and seeing different disc jockeys and being on the air, and then they'd play your record.

The relationship between artists and radio was phenomenal. There was a period of time in my life where there wasn't a city in America where I wasn't friendly with different disc jockeys and program directors. Radio and artists worked very tightly together. You really got to know each other.

But Dick Clark's *American Bandstand* was the most important vehicle for really breaking a record wide open and bringing it home. If you got on TV and he played your record, almost every radio station would follow suit. There wasn't anything more important.

How do you get a record played anymore? What do you do? Where do you go?

Dancing with stars. *American Bandstand*, 1968

❧ smokey robinson ❧

It would be impossible to overstate the impact of Smokey Robinson on American music. Anyone who's ever listened closely to one of Robinson's treasures, "The Tracks of My Tears," would know that the man could certainly turn a phrase, and when he used that velvety high tenor soul voice of his to get the lyrics across in song, well, the poetry of it all could drop a grown man to his knees.

Smokey Robinson is certainly one of the greatest soul songwriters and singers of all time. Early on in his career he mastered the art of writing and singing the love-soaked pop tune, one that was simple and easy to grasp yet contained enough poetic power to lock in a listener and have the song stay in the head and heart for a long time, if not forever. Robinson's music appealed to young black *and* white listeners, and that caused a seismic shift in American pop music.

He came along at precisely the right time—the late 1950s—and was also in the right place—Detroit—to meet the right person—Berry Gordy, Jr.—to launch a career that would shape the sound of soul music a few years later. William "Smokey" Robinson formed the Five Chimes in 1955 while still in high school. A couple of years later, in 1957, they had become the Miracles. Their set included a number of Robinson's original songs. That same year he met Gordy, a songwriter himself, and the two became friends.

Gordy would start a record company, Motown. The first act he signed was the Miracles. In 1960, Robinson wrote "Shop Around" and recorded it with the Miracles. The single went to number one on the R&B charts and, more impressively, number two on the pop charts. It turned out to be the tip of the iceberg; Robinson was just getting started.

Mary Wells, the first female singer signed to Mo-town, took a Robinson song, "My Guy," to number one on the pop charts in 1964, during the height of Beatlemania. Robinson with Miracle Ronnie White then wrote an "answer song" called "My Girl" and gave it to one of Motown's other groups, the Temptations, who took it to the top of the pop charts a year later.

Gordy had been smart enough to make Robinson vice-president of Motown as early as 1961, in effect securing his talents for the label and giving him a wide swath of creative freedom. Robinson didn't just write songs for his group and others on the label. He also signed artists to Motown (the Supremes, for instance), produced them, arranged them, and encouraged them to reach for the highest emotional peaks.

The list of Motown songs Robinson wrote is long. For the Marvelettes he penned "Don't Mess with Bill" and "The Hunter Gets Captured by the Game." He gave "Ain't That Peculiar" to Marvin Gaye. In addition to "My Girl," Robinson also gave the Temptations "The Way You Do the Things You Do" and "Get Ready." He kept for the Miracles "Mickey's Monkey," "Going to a Go-Go," "You Really Got a Hold on Me," "Ooo Baby Baby," and of course, "The Tracks of My Tears." When the group became Smokey Robinson and the Miracles, he added "I Second That Emotion" and "The Tears of a Clown." All were mega Motown hits. All are considered today super soul classics.

Robinson began a solo career in 1972 and never looked back. He's continued to record and perform and remains one of the stalwarts of soul, a pop poet in the truest sense of the term.

ON EARLY INFLUENCES

I grew up in a home where everything was being played. I had two older sisters, and they and my mom played every kind of music you can think of: gut bucket blues, John Lee Hooker, T-Bone Walker. They played classical music and jazz, Sarah Vaughan, Frank Sinatra, Billy Eckstine, Sammy Davis, Harry Belafonte, and Patti Page. These people were being played in my home all day long. My sisters loved the music they called bebop, and their friends would come over and they'd be dancing that jitterbug and listening to Charlie Parker and Miles Davis and Dizzy Gillespie and Count Basie.

I remember seeing films of Bessie Smith and people of that era, and what impressed me most was that there were no microphones back then. They were playing in these honky-tonk joints and in these blues places and stuff like that, belting it out. And everybody in there could hear them. They had a piano player and maybe a guitarist or maybe a drummer or something, but they were just in there, belting it out. And they had these big voices that resonated throughout those places. Jackie Wilson was my number-one singing idol as a kid growing up. I always tried to write songs. I had been writing songs since I was five years old, really.

At the time, radio was very important, especially before everybody started getting televisions. Radio was like TV. We would sit around and listen to the radio like people sit and look at TV now. Especially in the black neighborhood where people just didn't have money to buy TV sets, radio was huge.

ON R&B

The origin of all rhythm and blues music is the cotton field. Those people were out there, and they were working their butts off from dawn until dusk, picking cotton. The only entertainment that they had was to entertain themselves. So they sang hymns. And the hymns became the blues. They sang the blues because of the strife that they were living, and how their lives were going.

The blues was born out of that strife and out of those hymns. Then, later on, the blues became rhythm and blues. And it became pop. And it even became country.

ON MOTOWN

What made Motown sound like more than just black music for a black audience was Berry Gordy. Motown was started by a guy whose first love was music. He was a songwriter and a record producer and that's what he loved, that's what he loved doing. And so we had an advantage with him at the helm.

Berry Gordy had this dream, and it was a dream that would make other dreams come true. He had worked on an assembly line for Chrysler, and he had started writing songs on that assembly line. So he knew about building things, putting them together. On the very first day the company was formed, Berry Gordy said, "I'm starting this record company. We are not going to only make black music. We're going to make music for everybody. We're going to make music for the world. We're going to make music with some great beats and some great stories. And we're going to always do

"Berry Gordy had this dream and it was a dream that would make other dreams come true. He had worked on an assembly line . . . so he knew about building things, putting them together."

Robinson with Berry Gordy, 1981

Motown was a machine. And it was a very democratic company. Berry Gordy was a brilliant man because he never got in the way of creativity. Once you created something, he would critique it, and then we all did. Even Berry's ideas got shot down sometimes just like everyone else's. There were no exclusive relationships. [The songwriting team] Holland-Dozier-Holland had ten number-one hits in a row with the Supremes, but they were still open to other producers and writers. The goal was to get the best records out at any cost.

When Motown started to really become popular, people were bringing their acts from Kenya, from New York, from London, from Chicago and Los Angeles and Memphis and Nashville. They wanted that Motown sound, and it was right there, in the air in Detroit. And that was because of Berry Gordy.

ON MODERN RECORDING

Today people still go and buy records, and that is a really great thing. I'm very excited that vinyl is coming back. And they're selling record players again! The sound of vinyl can never be duplicated by a CD. There's something very mechanical about the sound of a CD as opposed to vinyl. Vinyl has a warmth to it that no other way of playing music does. And the album covers were great. I would read them to see what was going on behind this music.

I often think about people like Thomas Edison and wonder what they would think if they came back and saw somebody walking around with an iPod, a little thing with about a thousand songs in it.

quality music. That's our plan." That's what we set out to do, and we pulled it off.

We were like family, all of us; not just among the artists and musicians. The people behind the scenes and the corporate people were part of it, too. We even had family picnics.

Berry Gordy hired wonderful writers, musicians, producers, and artists. He told us that every song had to have a story, with a beginning, a middle, and an ending that tied everything together—just like a book or a movie. Even the people in the manufacturing department and in the sales department and in the promotion department had special talents.

The Miracles. *From left*: Bobby Rogers, Ronald White, Smokey Robinson and Pete Moore.

I don't think that all the new technology cheapens our relationship to music, or its value. I think music is a necessity, and I don't think it will ever not be a necessity. It is the international language.

I live a life that I absolutely love. I earn a living doing what I absolutely love. I still go to concerts and I still go into the studio to make records. And I write songs. It's what makes me happy. It's who I am. I have no idea what I'd be doing with my life if I wasn't doing music.

❧ ringo starr ❧

Once in an interview, Ringo Starr remarked that there were only four people on the planet who didn't experience Beatlemania the way everyone else did. "And you can guess their names," Ringo said, smiling. "It's certainly not hard to do."

It was an intriguing statement. By 1964, the whole world had been turned upside down by four lovable lads from Liverpool, England. Yet, to this day, Ringo Starr can't truly understand why he, along with John Lennon, Paul McCartney, and George Harrison created the cultural and musical hysteria they did. "Still hard to figure out," Ringo remarked. "Still a mystery to me."

What's not a mystery is the impact the Beatles had on, well, nearly everything in the 1960s. Hairstyle, dress, religion, film, politics, making records, Madison Avenue, merchandise, and, of course, music were all at least touched, but more likely transformed, by the Beatles. Simply stated, the group was the most popular, innovative, and influential rock group of all time. No one else comes close.

Ringo Starr, born Richard Starkey, joined the Beatles in August 1962, replacing the band's original drummer, Pete Best. Before the Beatles, Ringo had been a key member of Rory Storm and the Hurricanes, a Liverpool group that was every bit the Beatles' rival in Liverpool before Beatlemania.

As the Beatles drummer, Ringo crafted a drum style that was straightforward and simple, and left plenty of room for the lyrical and melodic genius of songwriters Harrison, Lennon, and McCartney to soar unimpeded.

Prior to Ringo, rock and roll drummers were often nameless musicians whose role in the recording studio was marginal and whose presence onstage was barely noticed. Ringo Starr singlehandedly changed the role and identity of the rock and roll drummer.

His sad-eyed glance, sharp wit, and endearing smile made him a favorite with Beatles fans, while his work behind the drumset inspired an entire generation of drummers, from the E Street Band's Max Weinberg, to Evan Jones of the band Fun. Even in the late 1960s, when drummers such as the Who's Keith Moon, Cream's Ginger Baker, and Led Zeppelin's John Bonham radically altered the style and presence of rock drummers, Ringo remained committed to the basic backbeat, keeping it on point and precise and offering a tempting alternative to the rhythmic excess and drawn-out solos favored by other rock drummers.

After the Beatles disbanded in 1970, Starr embarked on a long and successful solo career. Hits such as "It Don't Come Easy" and "Photograph" kept Ringo on the charts and proved he had a recording career well beyond the Beatles. Later still, he formed Ringo Starr's All-Starr Band, touring the world with it and almost always reinventing its lineup each time he took to the road. An acting career and non-music pursuits such as photography and painting kept Starr's creative juices flowing. A seven-time Grammy winner and twice inducted into the Rock and Roll Hall of Fame, as a Beatle and as a solo artist, Ringo Starr continues to record and perform today and very much remains a "drummer's drummer."

Beatles Concert
TIX ON SALE HERE!

THE BEATLES-LIVE-IN PERSON
CLEVELAND STADIUM SUNDAY, AUG. 14
7:30 p. m. All Seats Reserved
$3.00 $4.00 $5.00 $5.50
ALSO: "The CYRCLE" "The RONETTES"
"The REMAINS" - Othe Exciting Acts
RAIN OR SHINE - Don't Miss this Historic Show!

Jontzen ⬥ Cleveland

ON LEARNING TO LOVE MUSIC

As a kid, mainly what I heard were the songs everyone sang at parties. Music really didn't interest me until I was about thirteen. At that age, I was in hospital, and I was in there a long time—I had tuberculosis—so they had to keep us busy. Once every couple of weeks a teacher would come in with maracas and little drums and triangles and stuff like that. So they gave me a drum the first week, and after that I wouldn't be in the band unless they gave me a drum. I only wanted to be a drummer.

My first hero, at around seven, was Gene Autry. It was one of those magic moments for me: Gene Autry singing "South of the Border." I loved it! Then, when I was fifteen, there was an incredible magic moment when I actually left the hospital, and my family took us to see London. They took us to a stadium show where there were soldiers doing their stuff, and tanks—very exciting for a kid. Then you heard from out of darkness: *da-da-da-da-da, bah-bah, du-du-du-du.* And it was the United States Air Force Band and it was so great; that was another incredible moment for me.

We didn't really have a record player in our house until much later. We had radio, of course, and I was really interested in music when Johnnie Ray and Frankie Laine were around.

I was interested in music because of my family, because if they had a party, everybody had to sing. And my stepdad did great impersonations of Billy Daniels and Billy Eckstine. He loved big bands. I would be listening to whatever I was listening to and he'd say, "Have you heard of Sarah Vaughan? Have you heard of Glen Miller?" Bill Haley came in when I was fourteen or fifteen. He was another incredible influence. I loved American music from the start.

Soon I started going to the music shops just to look at the drums. My grandparents played mandolin and banjo, and of course they had a piano, but I had no interest in anything else, I just wanted to play drums.

First I made my own drums out of biscuit tins and firewood, bits of wood. The first drum I ever owned was a huge one-sided bass drum, which I used to entertain at the parties. And it was like, "Very nice, son." Then my stepdad came home one day with this drumset that cost twelve pounds.

It was all these old drums, and I started playing skiffle, a kind of improvised music that was popular in the UK in the fifties, but I was so stupid that I got rid of the drumset and got a brand new Ajax kit—because it was shiny, I suppose. Those really cool old drums—I'd appreciate them now, but then, I'm afraid, I didn't.

ON THE ENDURANCE OF
THE BEATLES' MUSIC

I think it's endured because it was so well recorded. And you know, we have to thank George Martin for a lot of that. But you know, we did our best, on every track, we

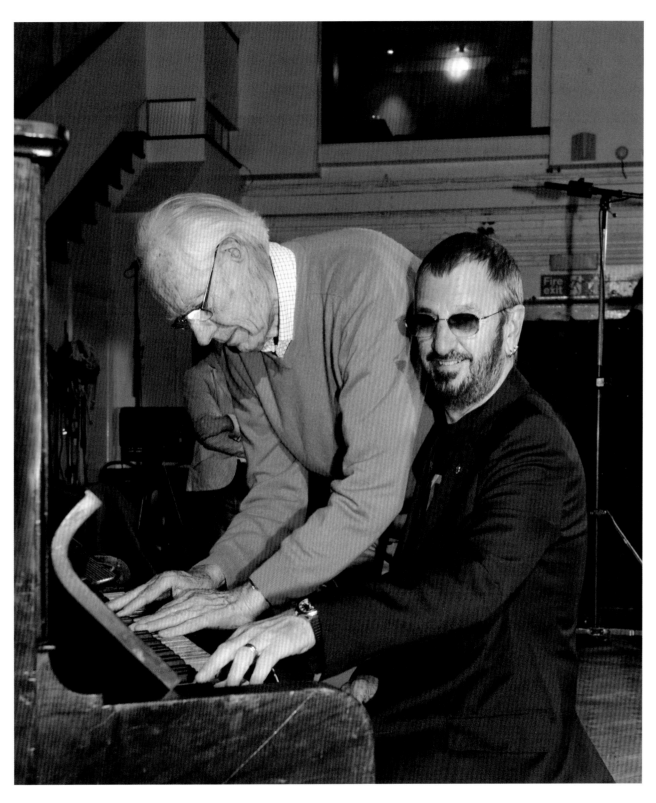

Ringo and Sir George Martin at
Abbey Road Studio, 2009

did our best. And George recorded it to the best of the machinery's ability of the day.

Then we mixed it, with the worst damn speakers in the world. And it still holds up because we always felt, if you get a good sound through those old Altecs, it'll sound good anywhere.

I think that's why it holds up, the feeling that's on the record. The record itself, the song itself, and the playing. That's the proudest thing for me—that it was about the music and it's still about the music. It was always about the music.

I loved music, I loved the drums, and I loved those other three guys. And you know, it's well documented that we weren't all loving each other as much as we should have. But once the counting came in, all of our craziness, emotional hurt, or whatever went out the window. When we heard, "One, two, three, four!" we just played to the best of our ability. No one ever jeopardized a track.

We all felt like that, not just me. We did our best every time.

ON GEORGE MARTIN

He's a genius.

When we first met George, we loved him because he took a chance on us. No one else would take a chance—with a name like the Beatles and you come from Liverpool? Not a chance in hell. I have great memories of the early days. The engineer would take us through the rehearsal, and then Mr. Bigshot would come in. George was a musician as well, so any advice he gave was helpful.

I remember one day we're sitting in the studio and we played a track and we just played it and we ended the song and we went, "Wow, that was great!" And we said, "Did you get that, George?" He says, "Oh, you wanted to record it?"

From that day on, the tape was left on all the time.

ON PERSEVERING

The message was all peace and love. We grew up together, and we supported each other, not just musically. In life, we supported each other. And then it ended and I wondered what I was going to do with the rest of my life. Then George Martin said we should do *Sentimental Journey* [1970]. Then suddenly I was on a B. B. King record, I'm playing with Stephen Stills, Leon Russell, I played on John's [Lennon] first solo album, I played on George's [Harrison] record. I found another big world I could play in, and it's been like that ever since.

paul mccartney

Paul McCartney has made his mark, and it's carved in stone.

Sometimes it's difficult to believe that the Beatles' tenure as a rock and roll band was so short, given the group's immense significance. From 1964 to 1970, incredibly, just six short years—that's what it took for Paul McCartney, John Lennon, George Harrison, and Ringo Starr to turn the world upside down, to shake up pop culture and pop music in such a profound way that we continue to feel the band's presence today, and never seem to tire of their music, even if much of it was written a half-century ago.

The Beatles' story is a familiar one. McCartney and the others were born and raised in Liverpool, England. Musically, they dined on early American rock and roll and something in England in the mid-1950s called skiffle, which was a British version of American folk songs using acoustic guitars and homemade instruments.

McCartney had additional musical influences: show tunes, British standards, and pre-war confectionary pop that by comparison to rock and roll lacked any youthful vigor. But McCartney's understanding of what made for a good pop hook came, in part, from such influences, and he put them to good use later on.

McCartney joined John Lennon's Quarrymen in 1956, later adding George Harrison. They were a skiffle group, but they moved quickly into rock and roll, thanks to the sounds they heard and loved coming from Little Richard, Buddy Holly, Chuck Berry, and other American musical pioneers.

The Quarrymen became the Beatles, with a few name changes in between. They woodshedded in Hamburg, Germany, bars, elevated their showmanship at the Cavern, a Liverpool club where the seeds of Beatlemania were first planted, and added the final pieces—Ringo Starr on drums, and Brian Epstein as the manager—and off went the band to change everything in its path.

The Beatles might simply have been a great rock and roll cover band were it not for the writing of McCartney and Lennon. McCartney brought much of the pop sheen and witty musical twists to the relationship, while Lennon provided the edge and angst that was found in the best rock and roll of the day. Neither was more important than the other in their songwriting success. The combination was definitely greater than the sum of its two parts.

No need to list the songs. The Beatles are a part of the world music treasury. We know their songs. They gave Americans rock and roll wrapped in a Union Jack. The music was clever, later brilliant, and always immensely original.

Paul McCartney has also enjoyed an incredible solo career. Whether with Wings or without, McCartney never failed to entertain us and inspire us. His music has always been about who we are, where we've been, and how to proceed into the future. Paul McCartney—pop tunesmith extraordinaire, maker of more masterpieces than we can count, a monster musician, and a master in the recording studio. The world owes Sir Paul McCartney a collective thank-you.

Paul McCartney, 1966

ON EARLY INSPIRATION

When I was a kid my dad got me a trumpet 'cause he'd played trumpet himself. I learned "When the Saints Go Marching In." I could play that and I could play a couple of little things and I liked it. I loved my trumpet, but I realized I couldn't sing with it in my mouth. So I asked him, hoping he wouldn't mind, if I could swap it for a guitar. And he said, "No, not at all," and he was quite happy. I probably was thirteen at the time. So I went to the shop and did an exchange and got a Zenith guitar, which I've still got.

Growing up, the music I heard was mainly on the radio—Cole Porter, Sinatra, and I liked Fred Astaire. "Cheek to Cheek" was always a big favorite. And I recognized the greats like "Stardust" and "When I Fall In Love." So I was brought up on that. My dad used to play the piano in our house which he incidentally got off of [future Beatles manager] Brian Epstein's dad, Harry Epstein, who had a music store.

My dad used to play things like "Chicago" and "Stairway to Paradise," and he used to try and get the Beatles to do those songs.

ON SONGWRITING

In the 1950s, American influences were starting to come in. We loved Buddy Holly. We loved Elvis—he was a god—but Buddy was more accessible. I tried to learn the riff at the front of "That'll Be the Day." I was like, oh God, and I think George finally cracked it and taught it to us all. We could identify with Buddy because he sang and played his own instrument. If you think

about it, there weren't too many people who did that. Eddie Cochran did that. Gene Vincent didn't. Little Richard did, but it was piano. Elvis didn't. And, of course, the artists themselves didn't really write songs. We were just on the edge of that—writing songs—so that became one of our big selling points; people had never seen that. It must have annoyed the writers, 'cause suddenly there were these guys—artists who wrote for themselves. This was not good. Lunatics were taking over the asylum!

I look back with great fondness for those years; it was very exciting. I remember when we started to write. We had written a few songs in Liverpool. John [Lennon] would come over to my house and I might have an idea that he'd help me fix and finish or he'd have something that I would help him fix and finish. So we had a few songs.

ON THE ROLLING STONES

I remember going to Charing Cross Road, and going past in a taxi, we saw the Stones—Mick and Keith—so we shouted to them, "Give us a lift," and so they gave us a lift. So it was me and John and Mick and Keith in this London cab. And we said, "What are you doing?" and Mick said, "Oh, I got a record contract, but we haven't got a single," 'cause they were blues guys and they didn't really write their own stuff at first. They just did blues covers. So I'm like, "Well, we've got one, 'I Wanna Be Your Man,'" which Ringo had done on our album, but it wouldn't be a single for us—we had other songs for our singles. So we sent it 'round [to the Stones] and that was their

first single. It was very exciting—all that rubbing off with other artists and other writers.

ON MUSICAL DISCOVERIES

Buying records in Liverpool with what little money you had, you realized the audience's point of view, how good the artist had to be, how decent they had to be and not cheat you. Because I remember buying a Little Richard record once, and I saved up and bought it. And I had brought home this record—you know, Little Richard! I put it on, and he was only on one track! The record said "Featuring Little Richard," but I hadn't seen that and I didn't understand that. So later, John and the band would always

say we must never do that. This is why we always had good-value A and B sides.

The early days were so exciting because the great thing was we didn't know anything and he [George Martin] was the grownup even though he was ten years older or so than us—not massively older than us—but we were the kids and George was the grownup, so we'd look to him for the information, the expertise. For instance, the feedback on the front of "I Feel Fine." John had left his guitar on by mistake and he had put it near the amp, and we didn't know what feedback was but George did. What's that? George said, "It's feedback." "Can we have that on the record?"

I remember we loved mono. We always

imagined mono as coming out of a transistor on the beach because that was sort of where we heard a lot of our music. The first time we ever saw two speakers in Abbey Road control room, we sorta went, "Two speakers—wow! Twice as loud!" That's when George explained stereo.

ON THE FUTURE
OF SONGWRITING

I think that whatever you do, you still need music, and for that you need people to compose it, and record it. I see songwriting students and I ask, "That's nice, where did you record that?" and they say, "In my bedroom." That's what kids can do now,

and it's a pretty good-sounding thing. Technology doesn't sound ropey anymore; it sounds pretty good. But no matter how good the technology gets and the delivery system, whether its going to be a computer or pulled out of the air in the future, someone still needs to write it, someone's still got to compose it, someone still has to make it up.

I said to my dad years ago, "Do you remember that song you wrote, a lovely song called 'Eloise?'" And he said, "No, no, I didn't write it. I made it up!"

So I think someone will always have to "make it up." Only the delivery systems and the recording systems will change.

> "The first time we ever saw two speakers in Abbey Road control room, we sorta went, 'Two speakers—wow! Twice as loud!' That's when George explained stereo."

OPPOSITE
Performing at Lollapalooza, 2015

❧ george benson ❧

The electric guitar was a latecomer to jazz. Although artists such as Eddie Lang and Lonnie Johnson supplied guitar rhythms to many classic jazz recordings made in the 1920s, they played acoustic models, which meant that what they played was often overwhelmed by the sound of the trumpet and trombone, among other instruments.

The electric guitar came along in the late 1930s and with it, so did Charlie Christian, who demonstrated the solo capabilities of the guitar in jazz—now that you could hear it. Then came a slew of other jazz guitar masters— Wes Montgomery, Grant Green, Tal Farlow, Kenny Burrell. Eventually, George Benson would be added to that list, but it wasn't just his guitar playing that attracted attention.

Benson, born and raised in Pittsburgh, Pennsylvania, became enamored with the guitar as a boy. In 1965, when he moved to New York, he met Wes Montgomery, his main influence, and signed a recording contract with Columbia Records, discovered by legendary talent scout John Hammond. Benson made some good jazz albums in the sixties, first for Columbia and then for other labels. But nearly all the interest in the guitar back then went to rock players. This, after all, was the era when Jimi Hendrix, Jimmy Page, Jeff Beck, Eric Clapton, Mike Bloomfield, and so many other young rock guitarists rightfully grabbed most of the attention. If you played jazz guitar back then, you had to at least flirt with rock in order to pay the bills. Benson made his living, but barely.

Not many jazz fans knew it at the time, but Benson could also sing. He actually began his career as a vocalist who also played guitar. But Benson wanted to be known as a musician, a guitar player, first and foremost—not a singer. However, in the 1970s, with mainstream jazz in flux, Benson began singing again. In 1975 he signed a recording contract with Warner Bros. and released an album called *Breezin'*, which featured Benson as a jazz guitarist and vocalist. It was a good move.

Breezin' became one of the best-selling albums in jazz history. It won two Grammys, sold well over a million units, and made Benson a major pop star to go with his jazz credentials. From *Breezin'* came the single "This Masquerade," a Benson remake of the Leon Russell song. It was the first single ever to hit number one on the pop charts *and* the jazz and R&B charts.

Benson saw his future and it had that special combination of jazz and pop he mastered on *Breezin'* written all over it. Not surprisingly, future Warner Bros. albums by Benson carried the same winning formula. Beautiful, soulful vocals, coupled with smooth, pop-inflected jazz guitar and great songs made Benson a jazz-pop superstar. Thanks to the path Benson blazed, other major jazz guitarists now had a shot at stardom, even if they didn't sing much. Pat Metheny, Stanley Jordan, Larry Carlton, John Scofield, and Bill Frisell are all in debt to George Benson.

Benson is still recording and performing today, and his legacy continues to grow. He was honored by the National Endowment for the Arts as a Jazz Master, and one suspects there will be more accolades to come before he's through.

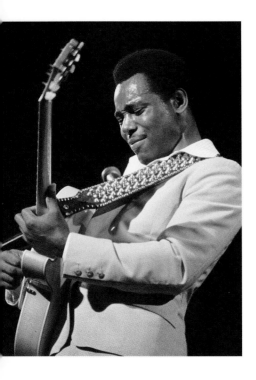

ON HIS FIRST MUSICAL INSTRUMENT

I was seven years old when my stepfather came into my life, and he brought with him two things that we had never had in our house: a record player and a guitar.

We lived in what you would call maid's quarters in the back of my grandfather's hotel. The place was probably built in the 1920s or 1930s, and it didn't have electricity. There were gas lamps, and we had an icebox that needed a big lump of ice to keep things cool. The hotel itself had electricity, but I never experienced it until my grandmother died and we took over the hotel. I remember that the first thing my stepfather did when we moved in was get his amplifier out of the pawn shop.

He plugged it in and I could not believe that the sound was actually coming out of the guitar and through a wire into a box on the other side of the room. Then he started playing, and the sound I heard coming out of the electric guitar was so amazing. That wire and box thing was just the most amazing thing that had ever happened to me.

It made a really big impact. At one point my stepfather left the room and told me not to touch the guitar. But temptation was too great, and I went over and plucked out three strings. And it turned out to be the three notes that made up the NBC theme. I felt so accomplished! When my stepfather heard it, he came back in and said, "Now you're going to have to learn to play that thing." And that's how he got me interested in the guitar.

He tried to teach me a couple of chords, but my hands were too small. So he found a broken ukulele in a garbage can and he took it home and glued it back together and

painted it. That was my first instrument. He taught me the first few chords, and in a few weeks I was out on street corners making money with it.

ON THE ELECTRIC GUITAR

The electric guitar is its own instrument. It can do things that an acoustic guitar cannot do. You can hit a note and you can rattle it or you can give it different kinds of vibrato. If you're Carlos Santana, you can hit a note that lasts forever, until you let it go.

Les Paul was influenced by Django Reinhardt, the greatest guitar player in history. All my conversations with Les have been about Django Reinhardt or Charlie Christian, who was the greatest thing that ever happened to the electric guitar. Les showed me all of the techniques that Django was using and how he only had use of two fingers on his left hand to work with to make the chords. So he needed to be heard.

With the invention of the electric guitar, for the first time in history, the guitar was not a background instrument. It could now take center stage, whereas it was previously dominated by saxophones and trumpets and other instruments. Now the guitar could be out front, and when it needed more power, you just had to turn that amplifier up and get the wah-wah pedals and do whatever you wanted to do. So it became a dominating instrument, especially in the rock world. When the electric guitar came along, it changed the way we made music.

ON THE DEFINITION JAZZ

Jazz is an intricate part of who I am. People always ask, What is jazz? I define it as four-four music played against a drum rhythm.

But that does not describe it entirely. Some people say it's a total improvisation. But if that's the case, then Jimi Hendrix is the greatest jazz artist of all time. So that doesn't really answer the question, either.

I think that jazz is a mixture of elements—including R&B, blues, and gospel—that has been put together to a particular formula that we call jazz today.

Jazz can be simple. If you're happy just playing against a four-four rhythm, you can do that and you'll probably have fans for the rest of your life. But if you want to grow, if you want to be a Charlie Parker, a John Coltrane, Archie Shepp, or Jimmy Smith, you can do that, too. Depends on how much effort you put in, how much experience you gain, and what you can dream up. You can grow and you can explode in any direction with jazz.

I used to believe that jazz was black music, that we had invented it. And a lot of people believe that. But one day, Art Blakey stopped me in my tracks and said, "Jazz music? We had a lot to do with it, too." He told me that jazz had been cultivated and brought along by many white people. And that's true of every form of music—it's all

made up of a combination of white, Latino, and black influences, with each having contributed their particular talents to the music. I have to give them all credit. Every race I've come across has a gift for something. And I think that's the reason why we're all still here.

As for the definition of jazz, I think Duke Ellington said it best. When asked to define jazz, he replied, "I can't define it, but you know it when you hear it."

George Benson at Albert Hall, 1978

❖ joni mitchell ❖

Joni Mitchell came onto the California pop music scene at precisely the right time. A few years earlier, she would have been cast as a young West Coast folkie whose lineage led straight to the likes of Joan Baez, Judy Collins, and Buffy Sainte-Marie. A few years later and she would have been musically homeless in Los Angeles, with both punk and heavy metal battling the oncoming beats of disco. But in the late sixties, a time when L.A.'s Laurel Canyon scene was flowering, Joni Mitchell was recognized for who she was: a Canadian-born pop poetess of striking originality, a songwriter with both vision and vocabulary, and a singer whose wonderfully pure voice could carry her songs to the highest plane.

Few female artists in pop have attained the status and respect that Joni Mitchell enjoys today. Though her early music fell, if a bit awkwardly, into the California folk-rock field, her later work initially confused critics when she seemed incredibly at ease delving into jazz and even the avant-garde. Her lyrics ran deeper and were more confessional than those of most pop songwriters, and her music carved a wide arch of cultural influences.

Los Angeles was an odd place for Mitchell to land in the late sixties, considering her legendary distaste for the music business. But Laurel Canyon was the creative hotspot on the West Coast after San Francisco had been overrun with pseudo-hippies and hangers-on after the Summer of Love in 1967. Mitchell thrived in Los Angeles. After making her name mostly as a songwriter—Judy Collins had covered her song "Both Sides Now" and Tom Rush had a folk hit with "The Circle Game"—Mitchell released her debut album, *Song to a Seagull* (also known as *Joni Mitch-*

ell), in 1968; it was co-produced by David Crosby. Critically acclaimed—actually all her early albums were critically acclaimed—Mitchell's debut recording introduced the rock and pop worlds to one of the most interesting songwriters to surface in the era.

Her next batch of albums—*Clouds* (1969), *Ladies of the Canyon* (1970), *Blue* (1971), *For the Roses* (1972), and *Court and Spark* (1974)—might well be the most impressive body of work ever produced by a female singer-songwriter. And while it doesn't seem right to point out Mitchell's gender, the fact is that back then, pop music was dominated by men. Usually, female recording artists who wrote their own songs either fell into the pure folk field or came from the blues world (think Bonnie Raitt). Joni Mitchell revolted against categories. She was an original; she became her own category.

What followed this intensely productive period for Mitchell was a series of albums that ventured farther and farther from folk and pop and deeper into jazz and avant-garde territory. Her 1979 album *Mingus* was artistically daring. Mitchell collaborated with the legendary jazz bassist, she setting lyrics to his music and then writing pieces herself. Charles Mingus set the stage for where Mitchell would go in the decades that followed, which was anywhere she wanted. She did more collaborations (Willie Nelson, Tom Petty, Michael McDonald), pursued more unconventional music paths, continued her exploration of jazz themes, stopped touring, and in 2014 released a career retrospective box set called *Love Has Many Faces: A Quartet, A Ballet Waiting to Be Danced.*

Joni Mitchell, 1974

ON LEARNING TO PLAY MUSIC

When I was a child we didn't have a lot of records, but my father was a trumpet teacher, and he played in small local swing bands. My mother loved nocturnes, so she had "Clair de Lune" and "Moonlight Sonata" and every romantic piano piece. Then there was the radio, which was pretty mixed broadcasting at that time. There was a lot of country and western music. I didn't really like it, and I used to make fun of it. But I loved Hank Williams and I knew all of his lyrics. Then in the fifties, rock and roll came along.

From then on, it was all about the jukeboxes in town. I became a lindy hop—or a jive or bop—dancer. And I went wherever there were sock hops or dances. They were all playing mainly Motown, the Platters, some Everly Brothers, Buddy Holly, and that kind of stuff.

I taught myself to play guitar from a Pete Seeger record, but basically, the only thing on the record that interested me was the first track, which was how to tune the guitar, and the last track, which was about finger picking. I tried to do it but I couldn't get my thumb to alternate, so I ended up with kind of a drone pattern coming off my thumb which is distinctive of my playing style.

One day there was a music festival at

Big Sur, and there was a girl there who built dulcimers. She gave one to me and I put it across my knee. The moment it went across my knee, as far as I was concerned, it was a bongo drum. The dulcimer is supposed to be plucked with a feather, and there's a certain way to play it. But I began to beat on it, and they kind of stopped me and said, no, that's not the way to do it, and then they kind of let me go. Well, that way of using the dulcimer influenced the way I play guitar; I used a slapping style, which I had seen other people do. So my way of playing came from the transition of going from dulcimer back to guitar.

ON WRITING SONGS

The first piece of music I wrote was called "Robin Walk." I wrote it out in notes, and my teacher hit me with a ruler for it and told me it was wrong to make up songs when I had the masters at my fingertips. The idea of being hit with a ruler at a moment of creativity—it killed my love of music for ten years until I was eighteen, when I took up the guitar.

When I started writing songs seriously, there were things about old standard songs that I wanted to keep. I wanted to keep a melodic sense, which was disappearing in my generation. I had a hard time getting some of the chords I heard in my head out of normal tuning, so I invented my own tuning, so that I could get a more sophisticated or modern harmony out of the guitar and avoid the clichés that were being cycled and recycled that didn't seem to bother anybody but me. At the time, women weren't considered to be real members in pop bands. The women were really kind of decorative. They'd treat them like party favors, in a

way, and the song lyrics were all written by men for women to sing, so they were sort of stand-by-your-man songs. They were kind of doormat songs. But a mentality was emerging in my generation of women; there was this vague sense of change.

I mean, this is a man's world. So the idea was to bring some depth and some insight into the songs and to avoid stereotyping women in the same way that blacks object to stereotyping.

Joni Mitchell, 1983

ON PRODUCERS

I'm a painter first. So to me, a producer is completely unnecessary. Mozart didn't have a producer. Beethoven didn't have a producer. When I began to record, most of the men were very resistant to taking instruction from a woman. And a producer is often a sycophant, a babysitter. If you know how you want to make your house, you don't need an interior decorator. Frankly, all I need is a good technician whose company I enjoy. That camaraderie is important, since we're going to spend a lot of time together. So they have to have some depth because I'm always philosophical in the studio. They

have to be able to enjoy that and not be annoyed by it. Some love it and some don't. So you have to find the right chemistry. It has to be simpatico, somebody that finds that a woman who's always theorizing and philosophizing is not a waste of time. When I got my first record deal I requested that I would not have to work with a producer for personal reasons so that I could continue my experimentation and allow my work to unfold organically.

ON BEING LABELED
A FOLK SINGER

I look like a folk singer because I'm alone with an acoustic instrument that's been associated with folk music. But if you listen to the music, you know it's not like any folk song you ever heard. Nor am I singing folk music, which is an antique. It's keeping a tradition going. I'm making original, new music with original, new harmonic movement, as fresh and as innovative as a young

Franz Schubert. My songs contain longer musical forms, they've got bridges, and the harmony is not based on the simple three-chord changes that typify folk music.

So I've always resented being called a folk musician. It was a shallow observation and it was also delivered with prejudice as something that is out of style. I like folk music, but the moment I began to write my songs, I knew that folk music was an inappropriate label for them.

I'm an outsider. I don't belong to anything. There's no pill that I can swallow whole. The Eagles, Jackson Browne—they have a harmonic kindredness and they belong to a school. I am not of that school. My thing is, I'm an individual as defined by Nietzsche: someone who can't follow and doesn't want to lead. I'm a fine artist working in a pop arena. I don't want to start a school and I don't want to belong to a school. What I want is to improve culture.

"I like folk music, but the moment I began to write my songs, I knew that folk music was an inappropriate label for them."

✦ michael tilson thomas ✦

Michael Tilson Thomas is one of the most prominent figures in contemporary American classical music. Not only has he been the Music Director of the San Francisco Symphony for over twenty years, making him the longest-tenured of all American symphonic music directors, but he is also the founder and Artistic Director of the New World Symphony. As a conductor and composer, Thomas has helped give American classical music a respected plot on the international classical music landscape.

Where other conductors and composers regularly stress the influence of and seek to interpret the great European composers—Beethoven, Bach, Mozart, and others—Thomas is known for his celebratory interpretations of Aaron Copland, Charles Ives, George Gershwin, Steve Reich, John Cage, and other American composer greats. Even his own compositions, principally *Poems of Emily Dickinson* and *Urban Legend,* draw from a distinctly American wellspring. Like earlier American classical music composers, Thomas has interpreted our national experience in a way that brings value to our culture, both at home and abroad, and, at the same time, proves that the American music scene isn't only about pop and roots music.

Thomas was born in Los Angeles and studied at the University of Southern California. Early on he worked with such noted composers as Stravinsky, Boulez, Copland, and Stockhausen, gaining valuable experience and inspiration. In 1969 he made his classical music debut in New York with the Boston Symphony. A stint with the Buffalo Philharmonic followed before Thomas became Principal Guest Conductor of the Los Angeles Philharmonic in the early 1980s.

Always an advocate of music education, in 1988 Thomas formed the New World Symphony, a graduate school of sorts for composers and conductors of prestigious music programs. Like Leonard Bernstein before him, Thomas embraced a responsibility to make certain American classical music had a youth base from which new generations of composers and conductors would rise.

It would be as the Music Director of the San Francisco Symphony, however, that Thomas would make his biggest mark. Emphasizing the interpretation of the great American composers, Thomas often presented their music in innovative and exciting ways, enhancing the symphonic experience for newcomers to classical music and bringing to life American classical music in ways that uniquely celebrated their contributions to the world music treasury.

Yet Thomas's interest in music goes beyond American classical music. He worked with the London Symphony Orchestra from 1988 to 1995 and has explored the works of Rachmaninoff, Beethoven, Mozart, Mahler, and Britten, among other European composers. Even Thomas's own compositions occasionally come from European ideas and concepts. *From the Diary of Anne Frank,* for instance, is an important work from his compositional repertoire, while his interpretation of Mahler's *Symphonies Nos. 3, 6, 7, 8,* and the *Adagio* from *Symphony No. 10* won coveted Grammy Awards.

In the end, however, Michael Tilson Thomas is America's most respected and consistent champion of our homegrown classical music. At a time when American classical music strives to keep pace with our vibrant pop tradition, Michael Tilson Thomas is at the forefront as he continues to champion the cause.

ON THE EVOLUTION OF MUSIC

Music to me is a kind of architecture, a kind of design, a map of the human spirit. It's a kind of dialogue between instinct and intelligence.

We live in an age now in which music is dominated by rhythm. Certainly a lot of popular music consists mostly of a very intricate rhythm track in which there may be some scarcely recognizable melody or harmony or baseline or anything else. But it's the rhythm that's driving it. It's attractive and it's beguiling and above all, saleable. This has not always been the case in music. Other eras in music history focused on other things—melody, harmony, a sense of quietness in music which was supposed to offer the human spirit a place to be nurtured rather than provoked.

I believe all music goes back to primal musical sources. That means that we lived simpler lives once and we had things to do in those lives, like plant and harvest and march off somewhere or whatever. And we had music in our lives for those occasions— they gave us the courage, the inspiration, the solace to deal with these events in our lives. And from those primal expressive urges in music, all kinds of forms evolved which we later called folk songs or dance songs or hymns or marches, things like that. And then from that music, we began to see larger musical ideas, the kinds of ideas that symphonies and sonatas and classical music forms are about. You can still hear the echoes of these primal village kinds of musics inside of classical music.

Isaac Stern used to have a way of playing some passages in the Beethoven violin concerto which reminded you that before there was a violin, there was a fiddle. And

that guys were just playing the fiddle. Even inside of a Beethoven concerto, Isaac could play in such a way that it was still Beethoven, but somehow, it was fiddle music.

ON HOW MUSIC IS PASSED ON

Initially, the way people passed music on was through an oral tradition. You heard somebody sing something, you tried to sing it as much the way they sang it, and maybe you put your own little spin on it and then you sang it for somebody else. That went on for a long time.

Then we had the notation of music. By writing the music down, you could much more exactly say things about the way the music was and consider many more complex relationships. Notation of music led to a kind of equal ground between instinct and intelligence inside of music. And the kinds of thoughts you had to think about music in order to encode it, to write it down, led you to different forms in music, different kinds of shapes, different priorities.

But now we have the technological passing on of music. And technology is way more impersonal a force than either oral tradition or notational tradition. Fine, there's a machine that does a particular thing.

Initially what it's done is to stack the deck way more towards improvisation. It's possible for someone who doesn't read music or think about it particularly to have a great world influence because the technology's taking care of preserving what they're doing and marketing is taking care of distributing it.

How this is changing musical thought, the way people perceive music, the way that people create music, we don't really know yet. It certainly is changing it. My biggest fear is that it's creating a culture of musical consumers rather than music makers.

ON CLASSICAL MUSIC

There's no good way of defining it. It's a musical tradition that goes back about 1,200 years or so. And since that time, it's been so many different things. It's been songs and dances and larger abstract cathedral-like structures built out of these kinds of little tunes, or it's been the development of harmony and all of its complex observation of the ambiguous, ambivalent nature of the human spirit.

It's been so many things in so many different countries that there's no simple answer, other than to say, it is a kind of music that abstracts simple things, a simple song, a simple dance, and puts them into a larger design in which they contend with one another to a larger purpose.

Popular music generally is popular because it comfortingly deals with one idea at a time. It's one groove, one mood, one thing. And you can kind of lock into it and it defines a particular moment.

Classical music, by and large, deals with many moods that may be contradictory in their meaning and which amazingly can coexist simultaneously. They're constantly testing one another and taking the measure of one another.

So the way you first hear them, at the beginning of a composition, may be quite different from the way they turn out to be at the end. It's like real life. It's like our real thoughts. Everything is being weighted and measured and reconstituted.

If you're alive, you have all the experience you need to understand and love classical music. You just have to have the opportunity to experience it. We live in a time where we have this illusion that we have access to everything, that we have this whole musical democracy which allows everybody a chance to hear whatever he wants. That's just not true. The material is there but people's access to the material is being very much spun by the marketing imperatives of recording companies or other large media organizations.

After many generations of this process, people don't really know any longer what is there or what, if they were left to their own free choices early enough in their lives, they might decide is important for them.

Classical music is still a very big deal for a lot of people. There are big audiences for it, there are young audiences that are developing for it. The more young people have a chance to experience the music when they are young, when they're getting their language skills together, taking on the language of classical music is something which they find a lifelong rewarding experience.

If you put on a Beethoven concert, you're going to have a lot of people showing up. Even though Chuck Berry said Beethoven had to roll over, *he ain't rolling over!*

Michael Tilson Thomas leading the Philadelphia Orchestra in Berlioz's 'Symphony Fantastique' at Carnegie Hall, December 6, 2013

"[Classical music] is a kind of music that abstracts simple things, a simple song, a simple dance, and puts them into a larger design in which they contend with one another to a larger purpose."

❦ eric clapton ❦

Eric Clapton came to the blues the way nearly every other young British musician did in the early 1960s: with awe, excitement, and an insatiable appetite to know more, make more, and learn *everything* about the African-American music form. The blues was exotic, fascinating, captivating, and Clapton learned early on that it was also deceptively simple. Its musical structure—mostly just three chords—was easy to grasp, as was the form's lyrical strategy—one line that repeated itself, followed by two shorter lines before resolving on a third the same length as the first two. But to play the blues with authenticity and with the emotional intensity the music demanded, well, that was something else again.

Clapton got his first guitar as a young teen. Interest in American blues soon followed. In late 1963 he joined the British blues-based band the Yardbirds, where his increasing proficiency on guitar began to attract attention. But when the Yardbirds steered closer to pop than blues, Clapton bolted, next joining John Mayall and the Bluesbreakers in 1965. The following year the band's classic recording, *Bluesbreakers—John Mayall with Eric Clapton,* made Clapton a certified British blues star. His guitar work revealed the influences of American bluesmen Freddie King, Buddy Guy, and Muddy Waters. Equally impressive, his penchant for playing solos that sought to honor the blues rather than recklessly reinvent them earned Clapton special status. Before long, graffiti could be seen around London announcing, "Clapton Is God."

Clapton's creative urge pushed him beyond Mayall and the Bluesbreakers. In 1966 he formed Cream with bass player Jack Bruce and drummer Ginger Baker, a band that beautifully blended blues with psychedelic rock. The trio format gave Clapton a wide field in which to engage fully the sonic possibilities of such an intriguing music hybrid, and his solos soared.

Although Cream was short-lived—it broke up just two years later—Clapton was now a superstar with all the pressures and responsibilities that came with it. Another supergroup, Blind Faith, failed after just one album. A stint with the American R&B duo Delaney and Bonnie came next, leading to the creation of the group Derek and the Dominos. The band's double album, *Layla and Other Assorted Love Songs* (1970), became a Clapton masterpiece. The title song might well be the most agonizingly honest rock song ever recorded.

Derek and the Dominos never endured as a full-time band. Instead, Clapton launched a spectacularly successful solo career in which he carefully balanced blues with rock and pop. What followed was a long string of hit albums, Top Ten singles, sold-out tours, and honors. Clapton was inducted into the Rock and Roll Hall of Fame three times—the first artist to achieve such a feat. Initially, he went in as a member of the Yardbirds, then as a member of Cream, and finally as a solo artist. He's also been inducted into the Blues Hall of Fame and the Songwriters Hall of Fame. "Music gives me sustenance, first and foremost," he has said.

Amidst all the great records Clapton made in the previous decades, he finally cut a long-anticipated true blues album in 1994 called *From the Cradle,* followed by a pair of 2004 Robert Johnson-inspired albums, *Me and Mr. Johnson* and *Sessions for Robert J.* These days, Clapton continues to perform and occasionally record, and always, the blues is the undercurrent to it all.

Eric Clapton during his tenure with Cream, 1967

ON EARLY IMPRESSIONS

I was raised in post-war England, where
there was a lot of music in the house.
American music was infiltrating England,
and my family were much more interested
in American music than English music.
We had swing bands and our own version
of everything, but it seemed to be watered
down a little bit. It didn't swing as hard as
Stan Kenton and Benny Goodman, who I
had been introduced to as a toddler.

Music was around in the house all the
time, so I heard Big Joe Turner and Jimmy
Witherspoon and those guys when I was
tiny. I think the first time I heard blues
music I intuitively made the connection
that this is where it started. I think I heard
Big Bill Broonzy and probably Sonny Terry
and Brownie McGhee, who were popular
in England even before I was in my teens.
Those guys were making TV appearances,
and their music was on the radio.

I think I identified with their music personally. I identified with the solitary figure.
It was one man's journey against adversity
that drew me. As much as I grew up with big
bands and jazz and swing and the Dorsey
Brothers and all that kind of stuff, when I
started looking for the purity of music, I
was drawn to the solo artists.

ON THE MUSIC
OF ROBERT JOHNSON

By the time I got to hear Robert Johnson I
had probably heard a fairly large proportion
of American black country music, and it
had been started with the guys who had
become commercially successful, like Josh
White, Big Bill Broonzy, Sonny Terry and

Brownie McGhee, Blind Boy Fuller, Blind Willie McTell, Blind Willie Johnson, Tommy McClennan. I felt drawn to the Mississippi Delta; it seemed like the hard core of musicality came from there. And so by the time I got to Robert Johnson, I knew enough to be able to listen. Somehow I knew that this was almost like the last thing I had to do.

That music scared the living shit out of me. I had never heard anything quite like it. And it seemed to me, the core of that was about the fact that there was no attempt to be appetizing, there was no attempt to be attractive, there was no gloss. That was such a shock to come across because all the music that I had heard up until then had contained some element of that. It was so raw and powerful.

At the time, we had a small group of guys and we would pass albums around—we were almost like reviewers. We'd take the records home for the weekend and then meet up on Monday and do our appraisal.

With Robert Johnson, we all came to the same conclusion. We knew it was good.

We couldn't write it off, but we also knew that we weren't ready. We were too young, we were too green, we were too interested in surface things.

We felt that we'd got hold of something that was just too primordial really to deal with. And so it became my mission to learn how to listen to this album. There was only one album then, it was *King of the Delta Blues Singers,* and it started with "Cross Road Blues." It was very satisfying and incredibly motivating to know that if you wanted to know what was going on, all you needed was this one record, and you would

find everything there. Everything that you thought you were hearing in modern pop music even down to jazz music of the sixties and seventies were on that album. Stunning, really.

ON EARLY BLUES RECORDINGS

When I started recording in the pop field, I was introduced to a studio with lots of microphones, and every instrument had an amplifier on it. I didn't know for sure, but on the Little Walter recordings I heard, I was absolutely convinced that the band was coming through his harmonica mic, because every time he sang or the band played, the volume of his mic dropped. Like it was mixing itself in as they went along. It didn't sound like anybody was moving any faders. And by the time I got to this stuff in the sixties and seventies, it had become so complicated and sophisticated that it was almost impossible to hear the room anymore. People were adding effects. On those early blues recordings, you'd hear echo being used, but a lot of the time, the sound was the sound of the room itself. There was magic in that for me, and I still go for simplicity in my

Eric Clapton's 1964 Gibson SG guitar, called "The Fool" and painted for him by a Dutch design collective of the same name. The guitar debuted in 1967.

own work and use as few microphones as possible.

ON FUTURE ARTISTS

Art is art, and there are always going to be people who are gifted, people who are dedicated to their art, and people who care about it for its own existence. And that can't really be tampered with. I don't think that's ever going to be in danger of disappearing. People are born with a gift to do something well, and as long as they understand that that in itself is self-rewarding, everything will be fine.

At his seventieth birthday concert, Madison Square Garden, New York, 2015

OPPOSITE
Eric Clapton performs at Royal
Albert Hall, 2015

❧ elton john ❧

On August 25, 1970, a young Elton John nervously walked onto the stage of L.A.'s top rock showcase club, the Troubadour. In the audience to see the singer-songwriter's American debut were some of the biggest names from the city's sprawling music scene, including Quincy Jones, Neil Diamond, Leon Russell, and Gordon Lightfoot. John's self-titled second album had been released just weeks earlier and there was a beefy buzz in the air.

Sitting at the house piano and backed by a small band, John beautifully worked his way through a set that included "Your Song," "Country Comfort," "Take Me to the Pilot"—all destined to be Elton John classics—as well as a riveting version of the Rolling Stones' "Honky Tonk Woman." The set was as perfect and as memorable as any debut could be, and when it was over, *LA Times* music critic Robert Hilburn predicted that John would become "one of rock's biggest and most important stars."

Twenty years later *Rolling Stone* magazine would call the now legendary performance one of twenty of the most important concerts in the history of rock and roll. Nearly a half-century later, Elton John is a rock icon, a master musician and songwriter, and a performer of such uncommon talent that his music is firmly entrenched in the world's pop music treasury, his stature as a performer renown.

The life script that Elton John followed wasn't nearly as ambitious as the results would indicate. Born Reginald Dwight in England in 1947, John began playing piano at any early age and won a scholarship to the Royal Academy when he was just eleven. Eventually he began playing at London hotel bars and such.

Things took a different turn for him after he met lyricist Bernie Taupin. Together they quickly became a formidable songwriting duo. Taupin would write the words and create the storyline, while John used his keyboard talents to invent dramatic tension with his music. The results were first heard on *Elton John,* released on Uni/MCA in 1970 to critical acclaim. (His debut album, *Empty Sky,* was originally released in 1968.)

Elton John became a regular on the pop charts. At last count he has more than fifty Top 40 hits, including seven consecutive number-one albums and nine number-one singles. His concerts were first held in arenas, then stadiums, and his persona went from introspective songsmith to rock superstar, complete with outrageous antics, dazzling stage outfits, and some of the wildest footwear ever seen in pop music.

The hits continued in the ensuing years. With songs such as "I Guess That's Why They Call It the Blues" (1983); "That's What Friends Are For" (1985) with Dionne Warwick, Gladys Knight, and Stevie Wonder; "Candle in the Wind" (1997); "Are You Ready for Love" (2003); the music he wrote with Tim Rice for the film *The Lion King* (1994); and soundtrack of the musical *Billy Elliott* (2005), Elton John's presence in pop music isn't just assured, but widely embraced.

Today Sir Elton John continues to inspire new musicians in his capacity as co-founder of the Rocket Music Entertainment Group. He is still a prolific first-rate entertainer with a life-long commitment to excellence.

ON THE MAGIC OF MUSIC

I was born in 1947, so I think the first music I heard was Bing Crosby, Frank Sinatra, George Shearing. My dad was a trumpeter in a dance band, and my family loved big band music. We heard Artie Shaw, Stan Kenton—very obscure music for a five- or six-year-old. Then the more popular singers came in, like Rosemary Clooney, Guy Mitchell, Frankie Laine, Johnnie Ray, Joe Stafford, Ella Fitzgerald. And a lot of classical music as well.

We had a piano in the house, so I used to sit on my grandmother's lap at a very early age—two or three—and play the piano. I used to be able to pick up melodies fairly quickly. I think the first thing I played was "The Skater's Waltz." Piano was always my instrument. I don't remember the first record I ever bought, but I remember going to the dentist—I had to have a tooth out—and bribing my mother. I said, "I'm not going to have it out," and she said, "I'll buy you a record." The record I wanted at the time was "Deadwood Stage," by Doris Day, and on the other side, "Secret Love." In those days the B-side was just as important as the A-side. I remember it was on the Philips label, a nice bright blue label. I got it after I had my tooth out, and I was extremely excited.

From the early get-go, music and records were so magical to me. I used to watch the records go around on the turntable, trying to figure out how the sound came out of the needle and this black piece of whatever it was.

ON DISCOVERING ROCK AND ROLL

There was a *Life* magazine in the barber's, and there was a picture of what I thought was an alien! It was Elvis Presley, who looked totally different than anybody I'd ever seen in my life. I'd never seen anyone dress like this, look like this, have a hairstyle like this! The effect these photographs had on me was quite astonishing. That very weekend, my mom came home with a record (she used to buy records every Friday after work). "I've just heard this record and it's the sort of music I've never heard before," she said, "but it's fantastic!"

It was "Heartbreak Hotel," and it completely changed the way I listened to music.

ON 45s

The 78 was big, and it broke. When 45s came in, they were smaller, and you couldn't break them. It was a fantastic kind of innovation. They never chipped and they never really wore out unless you scratched them. I was always so possessive of my records. I never lent them to anybody because they came back scratched and they would come back in a different cover. If a record came back in a different cover, it was like losing a relative.

Rock and roll had started with the 78, but the 45 really brought it to the fore. The first 45 I ever owned was "At the Hop," by Danny and the Juniors. With the advance of technology, the record player sounded even better. I remember stereophonic sound coming in. It was always a big band or something like that. It was never rock and roll, which was always mono. It was only when the Beatles started making records that I think rock and roll became available in stereo.

ON BUDDY HOLLY

Buddy Holly wrote some of the best songs ever. And he didn't look like Elvis Presley; he wore glasses. I had to wear glasses too, so he became a hero of mine. So I got a pair of black glasses, which I only needed really to see the blackboard at school. But because I liked the way they looked, I wore them all the time and my eyesight deteriorated because of that.

ON THE SIXTIES

There was an explosion of creativity in the 60s to the mid-70s of music that I don't think will ever be matched in pop music again. We were listening to Blood, Sweat

Elton John fashion, 2009

"I remember stereophonic sound coming in. It was always a big band or something like that. It was never rock and roll, which was always mono. It was only when the Beatles started making records that I think rock and roll became available in stereo."

A 1972 handstand on the piano

and Tears, Chicago, Frank Zappa, the Beatles, Pink Floyd, Ravi Shankar, Miles Davis, Aretha Franklin. There was such an incredible amount of amazing music being produced, from America and Britain. And the sounds at that time—technology—it started off with four-track, then it went to eight-track, then sixteen-track.

Technology wasn't racing ahead but it was certainly enabling people to experiment more as musicians. Everyone was willing to experiment with each other as far as fusing sounds, and genres of music were cooperating with each other.

It was an amazing time. Records were so important because you were listening to new sounds. When I heard the *Music from Big Pink* album by the Band, it changed my life. Hearing *Sgt. Pepper* changed my life. At the time, you could name twelve albums a week that suddenly would change your life because people were willing to experiment. The high musicianship, which you don't get now, was so incredible: Joni Mitchell, Leonard Cohen, Bob Dylan, Neil Young, Simon and Garfunkel.

It was such an incredible time of creativity that you'd sit there and listen with awe and amazement at all different sorts of music and try to incorporate them in your music. On the third album I made, *Tumbleweed Connection,* the song "Amoreena" is totally Van Morrison.

At that time, there was a feeling in the world of freedom; anything could happen, anything was possible.

ON SONGS

It all comes down to the song. If you've got a great song and you're a good musician and a good singer and you're prepared to learn and try and improve all the time, you can't really go wrong. It may take years before you write that song. It takes time.

We [at Rocket Management] have a Christmas lunch every year, and I say, "Listen, it's not important for you to get a record out right now. What's important is for us as managers to have faith in you, and that's why we signed you—to find the best creative process for you, find the right producer, get the right song. Brian Wilson didn't go from "Surfing Safari" to "Good Vibrations" overnight.

ON PRODUCERS

The relationship that an artist has with his producer is very important. The whole point of a producer is having someone who can say to you in the middle of a song, while you're writing it, maybe you shouldn't do that, maybe you should go to the chorus a little earlier. Or maybe the middle eight should be there. And I tell you what, when someone says that to you, you get so annoyed, because it's like, "It's my bloody song, stop interfering!" But the whole point

of having someone who can see the wood
through the trees is that you're so close to
it as a writer and you're so enmeshed in
what you're doing that you have to have
someone who's completely unbiased. That's
the whole point of having a producer.
That's why the Beatles used George Martin.
The Beatles were great songwriters—no
question about it. They were the most

brilliant songwriters. But they needed that
fifth member, and George was like a fifth
member.

ON MUSICIANSHIP

You can't rest on your laurels. You've got to
move forward. You don't bask in the days
that were. You bask in the days that are
ahead of you.

❧ yusuf / cat stevens ❧

Yusuf Islam was Cat Stevens, and Cat Stevens was originally Steven Demetre Georgiou, a Brit born of a Greek father and Swedish mother in post–World War II London, who came to be one of the most popular singer-songwriters of the 1970s.

As a youth, Georgiou fell for Greek folk songs and other traditional material before becoming enamored with pop and rock in the mid-sixties. He began writing songs, mostly for other people. Hits happened. American soul singer P. P. Arnold scored with Georgiou's "The First Cut Is the Deepest," while the English beat group the Tremeloes took Georgiou's "Here Comes My Baby" up the charts.

Drawn to performing as well as composing, Georgiou changed his name to Cat Stevens. By the early 1970s, thanks to hit albums like *Mona Bone Jakon* and especially *Tea for the Tillerman* (both released in 1970), which included the hit single "Wild World," Cat Stevens became an international pop star.

He had timed his ascent perfectly. The early seventies was a time when singer-songwriters played an important role in pop, and the introspective, soft rock sound of the decade dominated the airwaves and record charts. The sound of Stevens and other singer-songwriters, British and American, was in direct contrast to the acid rock of the sixties, which preceded them. It was almost as if rock had suffered a heavy metal hangover in the early seventies. Stevens and others like him toned down the volume, upped the sensitivity of their lyrics, and captured the art of melody without the long, convoluted guitar excess of just a few years earlier.

Stevens followed *Tea for the Tillerman* with *Teaser and the Firecat,* released in 1971. The album sparkled with two Top Ten hit singles—"Morning Has Broken" and "Peace Train," along with a Top Forty hit, "Moon Shadow." No one sounded like Cat Stevens. His voice, delicate and soft, playfully danced around his melodies and the unconventional rhythms that hinted at his earlier love of Greek folk songs. But he knew quite well what it took to write a hook, which made his best songs instantly irresistible.

Stevens would continue to release albums throughout the seventies, including *Catch Bull at Four, Foreigner,* and *Buddah and the Chocolate Box,* but with diminished commercial and critical results. Pop music was changing. Southern rock and progressive rock moved fans back to the music's louder and more complicated sounds, while disco and punk were on the horizon. Stevens, never comfortable being a pop star, refused to play the game. He lived for a time in Brazil, donated much of his earnings to charity, and began studying the Koran. By the mid-eighties, Stevens had converted to Islam, changed his name to Yusuf Islam, and had fallen off the pop music map except when artists such as 10,000 Maniacs ("Peace Train") and Maxi Priest ("Wild World") covered his songs and ran them back up the pop charts.

Yusuf Islam mostly rejected his earlier pop star life, preferring to work with children and release the rare recording. His double album, *A Is for Allah,* came out on his own Mountain of Light label in the mid-nineties; few in the pop world noticed. It wasn't until 2006 that he returned to the pop world in earnest with his induction into the Rock and Roll Hall of Fame and the release of the album *Tell 'Em I'm Gone.*

Cat Stevens, 1972

ON EARLY INFLUENCES

My father was Greek, so I had that kind of Balkan-ish background, and my mother was Swedish, so I had that Nordic element, which is very lullaby-ish. And then we had all the British shows that were coming into town. There was a place right across the road from where we lived that played South African music, which was a great chorus of vocal expression—very strong, based on the political movement over there. Then there was *West Side Story* and all these musicals. Growing up in London's West End means that you're at the center of theater—all the musicals came into town around the corner from where I lived. So *Porgy and Bess* was just up the road, and I saw the film *West Side Story* just down the road. I never had any inhibition about listening to any kind of cultural music. I loved Russian choral music, Africa and blues, even the old Irish jig.

My sister had a record collection. I was still young, maybe about twelve. She had money, so she had the records. I had been listening to Frank Sinatra as well as Tchaikovsky, and then suddenly along came the biggest explosive turning point of them all—the Beatles. My sister bought *Please Please Me,* which included "Twist and Shout," and that was probably the breakthrough for me. You know, it was like John Lennon's primal scream, *"Aaaaaaah-hhhhhhh!"* I think the first track I really fell in love with was "Love Me Do." It was so sparse and bluesy and yet English. The elements of their music created a new genre that I'd never heard before, like it had come from a different planet or something. It

was so different from Andy Williams, and Ray Charles was doing some fantastic stuff, but this new music was so against the grain.

I think everything has influenced me. I seemed to have a talent for being able to absorb and reinterpret in my kind of unique, quirky way what I was hearing at the time. I fell in love with R&B. I couldn't play it well, but I just loved it. But even from the beginning, when I picked up a guitar, I found it difficult to play other people's songs. I had to learn them, but I was just too lazy to do that. So I just started writing my own songs, and that made me happy.

ON RECORDS

The record was really important. That little piece of plastic was another way of creating a new universe that went around and around and around but always there was something new. Some new artist with a great new vision comes along with a new story and suddenly there's a new thrill. I definitely wanted to be on vinyl!

My perception of myself was changing, but I knew that somehow, I wanted to express myself. In the beginning, I had wanted to be a painter, a cartoonist, actually. So when I did finally pick up a guitar, I started telling stories and painting pictures with my words, almost from day one. And that was a natural evolution for me. I would say I'm a songwriter/painter. I paint with words and music. When it comes to light and shade, silence or sound, those are the things that I love to work with. And working with emotions. I think you can draw somebody in by being extremely quiet.

Cat Stevens performs in Germany, 1976.

ON RECORDING STUDIOS

I was always rather intimidated by the studio and all these sessions. Engineers knew what all the buttons meant and where the wires were going. I couldn't understand what that was. It was a spaceship; I didn't know how this thing worked.

So I was a little bit intimidated and I wanted to get control again of my music. The big change for me was when I said, "You know what? My little demos on my little tape recorder sound better than what I ended up with in the studio." So I looked for someone who could capture that raw kind of song that was within me, in the purest way, without interfering. And that's what Paul Samwell-Smith did for me as a producer. When we finally started making records, it was about stripping everything down to the most simplest elements.

ON BEING BARRED FROM THE UNITED STATES ON HIS 2004 TRIP TO A NASHVILLE RECORDING STUDIO AFTER HIS CONVERSION TO ISLAM

A lot of people have talked about this. I had been on my way to Nashville to record my first album in thirty years. And then this happened. This was not just an ordinary incident. But when I started meeting with police officers, it turned out they were all fans and they said, "We don't want to do this; do you mind?" And I realized that beneath all this, there was incredible support; that kept me going throughout the whole thing—immense support. David Letterman said, "We can all sleep better tonight because we caught the man who wrote 'Peace Train.'"

❧ mark knopfler ❧

When Dire Straits crashed the pop charts in 1979 with the classic rock single "Sultans of Swing," it was Mark Knopfler's desert-dry vocals and unique sounding guitar riffs that attracted the most attention. Then, after embracing both, listeners settled into the lyrics and found that he was a first-rate wordsmith as well. "Sultans of Swing" was a major hit, having wound its way deep into the Top Ten (it peaked at number four) and the eponymous album from which it came went on to sell more than twelve million copies worldwide. Its follow-up, *Communique* [1979], also went multi-platinum, and suddenly Dire Straits was one of the biggest rock bands in the world.

As a guitarist, Knopfler, a Brit, had drawn from an impressive well of influences. He knew the blues, particularly those of a pair of Kings, Albert and B.B., as well as J. J. Cale, Eric Clapton, and other stylists. Compositionally, Knopfler had Dylan down pat, and Knopfler quickly perfected the idea of song as short story. His best songs featured clever wordplay, but he knew it wasn't enough if you wanted it to endure a decade or so later. Knopfler, who had pursued a degree in English and spent time teaching literature, had the tools to write more complex pop songs, and he did.

Making Movies in 1980, *Love Over Gold* in 1982, the EP *Twisting By the Pool* in 1983, and the live album *Alchemy*

in 1984—all critical and commercial hits—were, ultimately, just warm-ups for the massive-selling *Brothers in Arms* of 1985. The acclaimed album produced three major singles: "Money for Nothing," which went to number one; "Walk of Life," a tune as irresistible as any pop tune could expect to be and went Top Ten; and "So Far Away," which slipped into the Top Twenty.

In addition to his role as singer, guitarist, and chief songwriter for Dire Straits, Knopfler was in high demand outside the band. He worked with Bob Dylan, Eric Clapton, Tina Turner, Randy Newman, Van Morrison, even legendary country guitarist Chet Atkins. His side projects included the Notting Hillbillies, a fun group whose album, *Missing . . . Presumed Having a Good Time,* was embraced by fans and most critics.

Dire Straits remained active until the mid-1990s. Since then Knopfler, whose reputation was such that he could do pretty much whatever he wanted, musically, released the occasional solo album (*Sailing to Philadelphia* in 2000 was one of the best of the bunch) and movie score. Knopfler, ever the laid-back musician who preferred to let his playing do the talking, continues to record and perform—on his own terms.

ON THE ORAL TRADITION

The oral tradition is everything, absolutely everything. One of the delightful things about it is the fact that it involved different people—poor people, whites and blacks working together, and listening to each other's music and being influenced by that. So the music reflected different cultures—African, European, Cajun, and everything else. So it's all this beautiful big melting pot of stuff.

Bill Monroe was once asked where all this music came from. It was this lengthy statement from some young academic, and when he finally asked the question, Bill just looked at him and said, "Up home."

ON GOSPEL MUSIC

I always valued the hymns that I learned at school. When you hear Van Morrison singing a hymn, it resonates quite strongly, and whether you're a religious person or not, you realize the importance of it, especially to hardworking people and the poor. These days they've managed to make it fit into the *Billboard* lists, so that now you have black gospel and white gospel. That doesn't mean much to me. When I hear Jerry Lee Lewis playing "Old Rugged Cross," I'm hearing tradition from the white side and the black.

Elvis is a perfect example of someone who was very much influenced by church music and by black music. In fact, he used to keep guys standing by, ready to play gospel music if that's what he wanted to do in a session. It's what he particularly liked.

ON THE ROCK AND ROLL EXPLOSION

Rock and roll, when it came along, was just a fantastic thrill. It was something that the

Mark Knopfler, 2013

"The sound of those guitars and drums followed me everywhere. I'd be at the back of the classroom, and it kept me hammering away on my desk at school, singing aloud, making the guitar sounds, and getting into trouble with the teachers for being this little one-man rock and roll group at the back of the class."

older generation were really against. I was still in short trousers at the time, and I was too young to be a rocker. But I wanted all that: the guitar, the motorcycle, all of those things. And I think that not having those things just ratcheted the stakes up a bit.

In the years before that, teenagers essentially hadn't existed as teenagers; the word didn't even exist. Back then, you wore the same clothes as your parents and then you got married. The girls wore twinset sweaters and pearls and the boys got suits like their fathers and worked in the same area in the same kind of jobs.

It was a fairly humdrum existence, and a lot of the records were just show tunes and moon-in-June rubbish. For adults it was very non-threatening. Then as soon as teenagers started to go out into the workplace and earn their own money, they could wear the clothes that they wanted and listen to the music that they wanted. It was a huge explosion going off all over the place. It was about breaking away from all

the stodginess of the post-war years. It was full of color and full of life and full of noise and this great, great whacking beat all the time and the sound of those guitars.

The sound of those guitars and drums followed me everywhere. I'd be at the back of the classroom, and it kept me hammering away on my desk at school, singing aloud, making the guitar sounds, and getting into trouble with the teachers for being this little one-man rock and roll group at the back of the class.

Before rock and roll, there had been no way for young kids to really let off steam. The older generation had been through a war and were very frightened and terrified. The world was recovering from all of that and just starting to learn to enjoy itself again.

Rock and roll came along just at the right time. For me, Chuck Berry embodied it all: that rhythm, the stinging little leads, the exuberance, and the use of the language. I think he was one of the first real great lyricists of rock. He used a language that was a teenage language. He was hip to the fact that young people really wanted this teenage explosion; he sensed it. And the songs that he wrote were all about that—sexual freedom and the whole new world.

ON NEW MUSIC

The way a kid makes a record today can come from any number of places; it doesn't necessarily come from the blues or from country music or from anything like that. There are kids now that have never heard of the Beatles. So their music will be influenced by the records that were in their own lives at various times.

And there's nothing wrong with that. You can't help but be who you are in the environment that you are in. But there are links in the musical chain that they may not be aware of. If they're interested enough, maybe they'll come say hello to some of those influences later on. If they're interested. There's no law that says you have to. It's like not expecting the driver of a car to understand exactly how the car works.

But if you want to play with some soul— and I'm not saying it's essential—you might want to appreciate the roots of the music, something that you might carry into your own playing.

ON NEW TECHNOLOGY

In many ways, old technology is superior, but I'm not against new technology and I use the best of it whenever I can. New technology's a wonderful thing. But what I like to do is combine it with the best of old technology. For instance, I might be using some of the latest converters, but I'll do it in conjunction with some microphones from the thirties and some instrument from the twenties. Maybe I'll use an old guitar from 1958 or something. When I have the band in the studio, I might try and record certain instruments—drums and bass, for instance—on tape, then transfer it to a modern digital system, and then edit that way.

What I find slightly amusing is the fact that as digital technology has become bigger and bigger, people are spending more time and more money trying to get that old analog sound with digital equipment. A lot of the early soundboards just had a wonderful warm sound to them. Very often, the best of the old works very well with the best of the new.

❧ bonnie raitt ❧

Bonnie Raitt might have been born to play the blues, but you'd never know it by looking at her. Red-headed with a sultry smile, sparkling eyes, and a pretty face marked by the occasional freckle, Raitt, as a young woman, seemed as if she had stepped out of a Mark Twain novel, running with the likes of Huck Finn and Tom Sawyer rather than the blues men and women she adored.

Add in her Broadway genes (her father, John Raitt, was a prominent actor who starred in *Carousel* and other musicals), her Burbank, California, roots, and the time she spent at Radcliffe-Harvard, and it's easy to see why Bonnie wasn't the typical world-weary blues woman. But few other blues artists—white or black, male or female, young or old—so deeply understood, loved, and ultimately presented the blues, especially Mississippi-born bottleneck blues, like Bonnie Raitt.

Like many other young people in the late 1960s, Bonnie Raitt found the blues fascinating, intoxicating, exotic, and illuminating. Even more, the music spoke the truth about the African-American experience and revealed the inherent struggle bound up in being black. Raitt embraced the sounds and songs of Sippie Wallace, Howlin' Wolf, and Muddy Waters, of Skip James, Robert Johnson, and Mississippi Fred McDowell. At first in her guitar playing, and then later, as it matured, in her voice, Bonnie Raitt became blues certified.

By carefully studying the best bottleneck or slide blues guitarists and befriending many of them who were still alive in her formative years, Bonnie Raitt became one herself. Eventually, her blues guitar solos soared and carried her own signature. Today, with all due respect to Memphis Minnie, Bonnie Raitt ranks as the greatest female blues guitarist who ever strapped on the instrument.

She signed a recording contract with Warner Bros. Records and released her eponymous album in 1971. From the start she was critically acclaimed; she was also an anomaly: a young, white, somewhat privileged blues woman with believable soul and sass. Other albums followed, though not all of them were studies of the blues. She explored pop and rock with varying degrees of success, broadening her fan base at a time when pure blues, in most circles, had lost its luster.

In 1989 she moved from Warner Bros. to Capitol Records and released *Nick of Time,* which would win her four Grammy Awards, including the coveted Album of the Year. Her follow-up, *Luck of the Draw,* won three more Grammys. But to call Bonnie Raitt a pop star would be wrong. In all of her music there was a blues undercurrent; you could hear it in the ballads, the love songs, even the rockers. Always lurking was the blues.

Many a Bonnie Raitt fan found out about Sippie Wallace, or Ruth Brown, or Charles Brown—all blues stalwarts—when Raitt acknowledged them. "They meant so much to me. From them I learned the real blues," she has said.

Bonnie Raitt was on the front lines in the fight against nuclear power in the late seventies, being a founding member of M.U.S.E. (Musicians United for Safe Energy), and she used her music and influence to stand up against social and racial injustice. Bonnie Raitt was inducted into the Rock and Roll Hall of Fame in 2000 and the Blues Hall of Fame in 2010. She continues to record and perform.

ON EARLY INFLUENCES

I was really lucky to be the daughter of a great Broadway singer—John Raitt—and my mom was his accompanist and musical director. He was the original leading man in *Carousel* and *Pajama Game* and performed in many Broadway shows for seven decades.

So first and foremost, I was the daughter of people who sang and played music all the time. My folks had a love for all kinds of music and exposed us to everyone from Mahalia Jackson to Ella Fitzgerald to Segovia. Being Quaker, they also instilled my lifelong passion for social activism. So it was a well-rounded background.

ON THE BLUES

Folk music was what turned me on to music. In the fifties and sixties, there was a folk music revival all across this country, and whether it was Appalachian music, Doc Watson, bluegrass, the English ballads that Joan Baez made popular, Woody Guthrie and Pete Seeger, the songs of the labor movement and civil rights—the blues is a subset of that.

There's just something about the blues, especially with the slide guitar, that's very expressive, almost like another human voice. And there's shadings of the way that you sing a blues scale, the way that you caress the notes, the way that you dig deep to be able to come to some sort of place in yourself that's either pain or longing or an attraction for somebody or somebody's broke your heart or you're angry or betrayed. All of that emotion is expressed in the blues. And that's what appealed to me as a kid, because when

you're a kid, you feel love and longing and unrequited love stronger than you do at any other time in your life.

ON THE INVENTION OF THE MICROPHONE

The amount of power people must have had to be able to project in a theater is inconceivable to me; I wouldn't have a career if it wasn't for the microphone. I can probably sing in a living room with twenty or thirty people and be heard, but the fact that my dad's generation and opera singers and popular singers up until very late in the game had to be able to project up to the top balcony—even over loud, noisy music in a jazz club—that's where you get someone with the power of Bessie Smith.

ON THE ELECTRIC GUITAR

When I met Mississippi Fred McDowell, I was like twenty years old, and I asked him why he went to electric guitar and he said, "Because when you play these clubs, you know, it's so noisy!" Electric guitar allowed you to play over the crowd, and with the slide guitar in particular, you can hold a note longer when it's electric.

Whether you're playing bottleneck or lead guitar or rhythm guitar, electric guitar is just so funky. There's all kinds of different colors you get out of electric guitar. It gives you more colors to paint with. It adds a whole other dimension of sex and danger.

ON THE HUMAN VOICE

There are people who don't have technically fantastic voices whose vocals have touched

Bonnie Raitt onstage at the Paradiso in Amsterdam on April 16, 1989

me so much more than anybody could believe: the vulnerability that they have just singing with three or four notes, the way the air comes out of their voices. And they're not thinking about it; they're just opening their mouths and expressing something. It's not about technical brilliance; it's just about connecting emotionally. I've had my mind blown by someone who says they're a bad singer and they've killed me with their vocal.

My vocal heroes are Aretha Franklin and Ray Charles, who for me are such incredible channels for every emotion. In one note Aretha can just shimmer between veracity and heartbreak and defiance.

And Ray Charles—his rhythm and his tone and his soul and his heart, they do the same thing for me. It doesn't get any better than Aretha and Ray Charles for me.

ON WOMEN AND THE BLUES

When I fell in love with the blues, I went back and got as many records as I could of the history that showed where this music came from, because I was fascinated with that. At school we were studying the twentieth century, and part of that was the birth of jazz—W. C. Handy and New Orleans and Fletcher Henderson and all that. And alongside that, it turned out the biggest stars of the day were the women blues singers, the classic blues singers.

The real germination of the blues to national prominence was the emergence of Bessie Smith, Ma Rainey—the classic women blues singers—Victoria Spivey, my hero and mentor Sippie Wallace, a whole slew of women that toured in what was basically almost like a vaudeville circuit in the tents on the Chitlin' Circuit.

For them, it was kind of a rough scene. There wouldn't have been a woman playing in a juke joint. It was just too harsh, and guys would hit on her or whatever. Memphis Minnie, who was a huge star in the thirties and forties, played on street corners before she had a recording contract, and she used to disguise herself as a man sometimes just because it was problematic. Women didn't move in that circle.

Sister Rosetta Tharpe was a great guitar player. And there's been great women jazz guitar players. They just don't get a lot of coverage. But they put out some of the biggest-selling records of that time. The blues really became popularized by these women singers. So there's a tradition of men and women singing the blues, and in fact, a lot of the Delta solo artists like Robert Johnson and Son House weren't anywhere near as well-known. Those women singers were the Beyoncés of their day, and we owe a lot to them.

ON MODERN MUSIC

The thing that's so great about music today is that YouTube makes it possible for someone to read or hear about something in an interview and then immediately go check it out. You can just see who all these blues influences are, and all these jazz guys, and

"Memphis Minnie, who was a huge star in the thirties and forties, played on street corners before she had a recording contract, and she used to disguise herself as a man sometimes just because it was problematic. Women didn't move in that circle."

Alicia Keys and Bonnie Raitt at the Staples Center in Los Angeles, California, 2012

see footage on Django Reinhardt. I don't know how anybody gets any sleep, because everything's available! And it's creating an eclectic approach to music that is so thrilling. There are hybrids of things going on now that we couldn't have even imagined twenty years ago, and I thought we were all pretty eclectic back then.

I made myself learn how to use Garage Band and then I got Protools. You know how I wrote half my latest album? On my phone! I just put the phone down and I played to it. I couldn't overdub, but then I played it through the sound system, recorded it again, and sang the second part. I've got expensive microphones in my guest bedroom that I could go whip out and set up the whole system with my laptop, but forget it, you know?

But I'm a dinosaur compared to what the next generation is coming up with. They're drawing from every kind of music,

and putting it out in a fresh way. They're not just retro. Which is really great. It's inspirational for me. I'm looking to the younger generation for inspiration now.

ON THE POWER OF MUSIC

For me, music is so expressive of who I am, what I need, what I feel, what I miss. Maybe it's because I was blessed to grow up in a musical family. But everybody has music in them. Everyone can sing; whether they want to sing in front of people—it doesn't matter. But there are very few people that aren't incredibly moved by music of some kind.

When I hear John Prine or Jackson Browne or John Raitt or Sippie Wallace or Bessie Smith, there's something chemical that happens in my soul. I'm drawn to it, and that's what music is for me. I can't imagine a life without it. It inspires me. It soothes me. It tickles me. It urges me on.

❧ tom petty ❧

Tom Petty fans know the obvious: Tom Petty *is* American rock and roll. Not one to push things by expanding its definition or aligning it with other music forms, or creating it on computers, for that matter, Tom Petty plays rock and roll, pure and simple, and we are forever grateful for that.

Petty's penchant for guitar-driven rock has paid off handsomely. In 2002 he and his band, the Heartbreakers, were inducted into the Rock and Roll Hall of Fame. His albums have sold in the many millions, he's played arenas around the world since the late seventies, and his ability to still record and tour, despite nearly a half-century in the business, is testament to his belief that rock and roll is more than music. For Petty and those like him, it is also a mindset, an attitude, a way of life that's celebrated and elevated every time a great band takes the stage and plugs in.

He was born and raised in Florida. In 1975 Petty's band Mudcrutch morphed into the Heartbreakers. In 1976 the group released its self-titled debut album. Far from soaring up the charts, the album sputtered along until the singles "Breakdown" and "American Girl" were discovered by rock radio listeners. Petty and the Heartbreakers released the follow-up album *You're Gonna Get It!* in 1978; it produced a pair of solid singles: "Listen to Her Heart" and "I Need to Know." Neither of them broke the Top Ten, nor were instant smashes. Instead, Petty's songs seemed designed to slowly but surely make an impression. By the turn of the decade, Tom Petty and the Heartbreakers had laid the foundation for success with simple, straight-ahead, honest rock and roll. They were now poised for the breakout.

It came with *Damn the Torpedoes* in 1979, which went

platinum, peaking at number two on the album charts. From it came the singles "Don't Do Me Like That," "Even the Losers," "Here Comes My Girl," and "Refugee." The 1980s and 1990s saw much of the same: hard-driving albums that sold well and scored critically and singles that reflected the band's rock and roll soul. In 1981, Petty and Fleetwood Mac singer Stevie Nicks had a major hit with "Stop Draggin' My Heart Around," which appeared on Nicks's solo album *Bella Donna.*

On the surface it was all so simple and even predictable: Petty would release an album full of great songs and then the band would tour and then rest a bit and then they'd do it all over again. Classic rock albums such as *Full Moon Fever* and *Wildflowers* highlighted his growing catalog. Petty didn't yearn for the spotlight, didn't carry on like the full-on rock star he was. He went about his business.

Then Petty shook things up when he joined the Traveling Wilburys with producer friend Jeff Lynne. The supergroup included Bob Dylan, George Harrison, and Roy Orbison, and fans loved it. The debut album, *Traveling Wilburys, Vol. 1,* was full of wonderful music and demonstrated that when egos were left at the door of the recording studio magical things might happen. *Traveling Wilburys, Vol. 3* (there was no volume 2) was more of the same. Who knows how long the Wilburys might have "traveled" had not the deaths of first Roy Orbison and later George Harrison ended a beautiful thing.

Tom Petty, however, pushes on. One of rock's most consistent artists in sound, style, and substance, Petty is and will remain the poster boy for rock and roll, the basic kind, the true kind.

Tom Petty, 1977

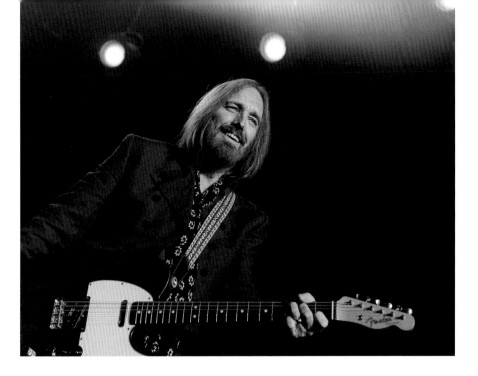

Performing in 2014

ON FIFTIES RADIO

In 1959, 1960, you kept in touch with the music world via radio. There was usually only one station. But it played everything. If there was a big country hit, that played. If Frank Sinatra had a big song out, that played. And if the Yardbirds had a big song out, that played. They might even play right next to each other. No one was worried about whether they were jumping formats. They were just playing the songs that everyone liked. It was fantastic. It was just fantastic. Imagine that.

ON PRODUCERS

The producer is the guy that keeps a close eye on the material. His job will be thankless, unless there's good material. He knows that, and he tries to make sure that the piece of music that you're recording is good and strong. You can make the greatest mix of sounds, but it won't add up to anything if there's not a good song there. There has to be a song or nothing's gonna happen.

So that's the producer's first job. His next job is to get the best out of the artist, create an environment where the artist feels comfortable, and you can actually draw the best out of them, their best perfor-

mance. Studios can be cold and intimidating if you're not used to them.

I think when people start to do multiple takes in a studio—I mean, when you're up to a ridiculous amount of takes—and you're still not getting what you want, a lotta people wanna push this far into the night and into the morning. The producer's job should be to know when you've hit it, and his ear should be trained to know when he hears the take that's *the* take, because artists just don't always know. They rely on the producer to guide them to it. It's a big, big job and carries enormous responsibility. The producer should also know his people, the artist that he's working with, their characteristics, their temperament, and how to keep that session flowing.

Typically, things are going really great, and then someone says, "Well, I've gotta tune the twelve-string," which we all know means "hour break," because they're complicated, and it takes a little time to tune them. A good producer will know that the twelve string's coming, and he'll have someone tuning that guitar and setting up that amp while he's doing the previous track. So the session keeps moving. When a session stops, and there's nothing going on for long periods of time, people drift.

OPPOSITE: At the Palladium,
New York, 1979

The performance drifts, and then you have to get that singer back into character. Very few recording artists know how to do that. It's not the nature of a musician. So the producer should keep the session moving in a way that's comfortable for the artist.

Most important, the producer has to be that outside voice, that critical view.

ON THE INFLUENCE OF BOB DYLAN

Bob Dylan opened doors to so many things, and singing was one of them. When I first heard him sing I was shocked by it, like most people, and thought, What is that? He's not singing. He's . . . is he speaking? No. He's not really speaking. *What is he doing?* It was so totally original. And then I became enamored of it and just loved it. And I realized, yes, he's singing, and he's singing really well, and he's singing right in tune.

That enabled people like me to have the courage to take a shot at it. I had been trying to sing things in my band. We were just a cover band, so we played the hits:

the Stones, the Beatles, the Animals, the Kinks, all the Motown stuff, James Brown, the Byrds. There were so many things going on, and so my voice became kind of a blend of all of that. And then I started to strip away the influences, slowly, and I found that I'd created something, and that something was me.

There are a lotta singers that weren't conventional voices, but [because of Bob Dylan] they were suddenly singing, and it was working, and we believed them because, really, all a good vocalist does is make you believe them. Whether it be Bing Crosby or Doris Day or Eric Burdon or Joey Ramone, you believe them. And when you believe them, that's a good vocalist.

ON TIME

Old people always think their time, their music, was better. Mine actually was! You know what I mean? Like, I'm an old guy, but I ain't stupid. If hear something that everyone likes, I can usually find something to like about it. But my time was better. There was better music!

With Bob Dylan at London's Wembley Arena, 1987

stevie van zandt

Stevie Van Zandt has more nicknames than most rock stars would ever need, or want. Miami Steve, Sugar Miami Steve, and Little Steven come to mind. If you're a *Sopranos* fan, then you might know him as Silvio, the character he played in the award-winning television series. In the end, though, nicknames matter far less than fact: Stevie Van Zandt is a rock and roll renaissance man. He's also, arguably, one of the most underrated artists in rock today.

Van Zandt is a longtime member of Bruce Springsteen's E Street Band, a guitarist and backup vocalist to the Boss. He is also one of the resident rock and roll historians in the band (along with drummer Max Weinberg and bass player Garry Tallent) whose passion for the history of the music is as strong and as deep as that of any music nerd holed up in a basement or bedroom with shelves full of vinyl.

He wears a trademark head scarf, and at times he speaks like the gangster he played on television. He'll tell you about the importance of preserving the history of the music and why it needs to be studied seriously in schools across America. "That music is who we are," says Van Zandt. "It's in the soul of America, and we can't forget that."

Van Zandt grew up on the Jersey Shore with Springsteen and most of the other E Streeters. He listened to the Rolling Stones and other British Invasion bands, and was hooked. He got a guitar, joined a band, and soon got good enough to play with the Jersey shore's best, including Springsteen.

Van Zandt formed Southside Johnny and the Asbury Jukes in the early 1970s with his friend Johnny Lyon. He wrote, produced, and arranged much of their material. The Jukes became the house band at the famed Stone Pony club in Asbury Park, New Jersey, and quickly resurrected the horn-drenched sound of 1960s blue-eyed soul.

Then Springsteen called and asked Van Zandt to join the E Street Band, just as he was creating his masterpiece, *Born to Run*. Van Zandt became a critical part of the band, often interacting with Springsteen on stage in a way that revealed their close kinship.

In 1984, Van Zandt left the E Street Band to start a solo career. He spearheaded the movement in rock and roll to end apartheid in South Africa with the production of the hit single "Sun City." He also masterminded a new band, Little Steven and the Disciples of Soul, which was Juke-based, but with more edge and attitude. Still, in 1995, he'd find his way back to E Street, where he still resides.

Along his rock and roll journey, Van Zandt has been a guitarist, singer, songwriter, arranger, producer, social activist, actor, record company owner (Wicked Cool), disc jockey (*Little Steven's Underground Garage* on Sirius XM), educator, lecturer, music historian, foundation head (Rock and Roll Forever Foundation), Rock and Roll Hall of Fame inductee, company head (Renegade Nation), Broadway musical producer (*Once Upon a Dream*, 2013), and music supervisor (*Not Fade Away*, 2012). Not only did he star in the television show *Lilyhammer*, he also wrote the script, directed the music, and produced the program. "I'm just getting warmed up," he laughs. You can't help but believe him.

ON THE ORIGINS OF MULTITRACKING

My generation considers Frank Sinatra the first real rock star, especially in the Italian-American community. But actually before Frank there was Bing Crosby, who was the biggest movie star, the number-one recording star, and the number-one radio star all at the same time. He had a radio show but it was inconvenient for him. He had recorded live, which meant he had to go into a studio and that cramped his style. He would rather be playing golf.

Then he heard about a guy named Jack Mullen, an engineer in the army stationed in London during the war. His job was to listen in on the Germans, eavesdrop on their radio transmissions, and try to figure out what they were up to. Mullen noticed that the Germans were broadcasting symphonies throughout the night. He wondered, Is Hitler so crazy he's having the Berlin Philharmonic come in and play at three in the morning?

He realized they must have invented some new kind of recording technology and indeed they had. They had invented magnetic tape recording. Up until then all radio shows were broadcast live. So the war ends and Mullen goes and finds one of these recording machines in Germany.

It was called a magnetophone, about the size of a Buick. Bing Crosby hears about it. The quality of the recording was fantastic, indistinguishable from a live broadcast. This new recording device would enable Bing to pre-record his radio shows, which meant he could play as much golf as he wanted to. And because it was recorded on tape they could edit the show to any length, make it perfect before they aired it. It became widely known that Bing was using this new invention for his radio show, but then he started using magnetic tape to record his albums (up until then all recordings were done to disc). And it wasn't long after that all the record labels followed suit.

Around this time Bing gives one of these magnetic tape recorders to his buddy Les Paul. Les Paul was a tinkerer. He loved to take things apart, see how they worked, improve them, see what they could do. So he was fooling around with this tape recorder and he figures out a way to lay down multiple signals on the same tape. And he winds up inventing multitrack recording, which would again change everything.

ON HOW THE ROCK AND ROLL UNIVERSE WAS CREATED

The Big Bang occurred on February 9, 1964. The Beatles played the *Ed Sullivan Show,* the big variety show that the whole family used to watch together on their little TV sets. I think that's probably what turned most people on to this new world called rock and roll.

At the time I was buying singles like any kid would. But I never connected to the artist through the records, oddly enough. I think I was weird that way. For me, a record was a record and I never really cared to go see the artist or who the artist was or anything—until that fateful night. I had a few great singles: "Duke of Earl," the Four Seasons records, "Pretty Little Angel Eyes," "Palisades Park," "The Bristol Stomp," things like that. I was an outcast misfit and

Ed Sullivan introduces the Beatles, February 9th, 1964

a freak and looking for somewhere to fit in, in the world. And suddenly, this new world appeared on television. Seventy-three million people saw it. And most of my generation, I think, was affected by it.

All through the fifties and early sixties we had great radio in America. People tend to look back now and think that our great radio began with FM radio, which didn't come along until much later. In the early sixties we had the AM stations. And rock and roll slowly took over and became pop music. They were not one and the same in the fifties. Rock and roll was this new sort of sub-genre creeping in. It was a wonderful time to grow up, probably the only time in history when the best music being made was also the most commercial.

With Bruce Springsteen, 1975

actually tell the truth! We can talk about our own lives! That was something people really didn't do very much. But now here's Dylan actually throwing in something that certainly seemed autobiographical or at least topical. And all that was coming from the tradition of protest music—basic folk, folk blues. So you apply real-life lyrics to rock and roll and out comes "Satisfaction" with the Stones and "Help!" and "You've Got to Hide Your Love Away," all these wonderful things. The art form had been born—the Byrds with "Mr. Tambourine Man," Dylan's "Like a Rolling Stone," Otis Redding, the Beatles. And from then on, things were more sophisticated and the priority of making it dance music started to change. It became more about listening to it and having a personal relationship with it. And an art form was born.

ON THE ROOTS OF ROCK AND ROLL

Rock and roll is a unique genre in that it has the ability to absorb and use all other genres, which makes it the most interesting, in my opinion, and the longest-running popular music of all the pop musics of the century. Why? Because it was so flexible. That's where all rock subgenres came from—folk rock, jazz rock, art rock, progressive rock, this rock, that rock. All legitimate, because rock and roll was able to absorb and use these things.

If we go back to the roots of rock and roll, back to the country blues guys, it very much reflects the history of America in the twentieth century—the plantations, immigration, the civil rights movement, the anti-war movement, the women's movement, as reflected by what was going on with

Then along came Bob Dylan, bringing in real-life words from the folk tradition and the country blues tradition into popular music. Everybody heard him. He played England and they all were there. He was just very, very impressive, and he single-handedly changed the world. Everyone picked up on those lyrics. Hey, we can

women like Grace Slick and Janis Joplin and going back to Bessie Smith and Billie Holliday. It's a wonderful way of teaching kids history.

ON THE TROUBLE WITH
MUSIC TECHNOLOGY

All through the fifties and right through the mid-sixties you pretty much recorded live.

The songs could be overdubbed, but they'd have to record what you did onto another whole machine, which they didn't want to do too often because it began to affect the quality of the sound. It wasn't really until '68, '69, and the 70s that the eight-track and then the sixteen-track was used. And this, of course, allowed you to play around a bit more. There were a lot of amazing things going on there and they would just bounce it down, bounce it down.

But these extra tracks took a long time, which was unfortunate. Records that were taking weeks to record now took months and sometimes years, because of the endless "let's try this, let's try that," and you didn't have to make a decision until later.

So everybody started losing their discipline and their ability to make decisions, and people started to focus too much on every little thing. Some good came out of these things, and some bad.

But now everything is digital, which is a bunch of numbers on a computer. It sounds very different. And I think the digital domain is missing vital information. Listen to your favorite vinyl record from the old days next to a CD and you'll hear the difference. It's a vast difference. Analog frequencies interact with each other, there's resonance, there's harmonics. There's this very wonderful mess of frequencies. Digital cleans all that up and puts everything very cleanly in its own place. But in my opinion, music wasn't meant to be that clear. Clarity is not necessarily a good thing. The truth of the matter is, art is like religion. It is most effective when there is an element of mystery in it. You want to leave room for people to fill in their own sort of imagination somehow and participate in the art form, participate in the religion.

"Listen to your favorite vinyl record from the old days next to a CD and you'll hear the difference. It's a vast difference. Analog frequencies interact with each other, there's resonance, there's harmonics. There's this very wonderful mess of frequencies. Digital cleans all that up and puts everything very cleanly in its own place."

❧ rosanne cash ❧

Her surname suggests country music royalty. Johnny Cash, her father, was King of Country for much of his career, his one true rival in the history of the music being the legendary, honky-tonkin' heavyweight Hank Williams.

With family ties like that you might have expected Rosanne Cash to flee from music, or else, to carry a heavy burden of country music expectations and accomplishment. Cash didn't run or cave in to all that pressure. Instead, she has managed the weight by being, well, Rosanne Cash, an artist of uncommon integrity and talent, one who has shouldered her lineage with dignity and respect, and, along the way, cut a musical path of her own.

Cash didn't go directly into country music. Although she worked for a time with her father, Rosanne spent time in Europe, attended Vanderbilt University in Nashville, and married singer-songwriter Rodney Crowell. Then, in 1979, she signed a recording contract with Columbia Records; a year later the company released her American debut recording, *Right or Wrong*. But it was her followup album, *Seven Year Ache,* that solidified Cash's country music career. The 1981 album garnered rave reviews and yielded Cash her first number-one country hit with the album's title track.

The 1980s saw a number of Rosanne Cash triumphs. Commercially successful tours, critically acclaimed albums, and number-one singles, including "I Don't Know Why You Don't Want Me" (1985); "Never Be You" (1985); "Tennessee Flat Top Box" (1987); "The Way We Make a Broken Heart" (1987); "If You Change Your Mind" (1987); "Runaway Train" (1987); and "I Don't Want to Spoil the Party" (1989), made her a certified country music star.

However, it wasn't until Cash relocated to New York and released perhaps her most memorable artistic achievement in the recording studio, the 1990 self-produced *Interiors,* that Cash's songwriting talents truly flowered. *Interiors* ignited Cash's earlier commerical success in mainstream country. Her ability to write candidly and compellingly about relationships, personal torment, and emotional turmoil gave her music a brutal honesty. Now known as one of pop music's top singer-songwriters, Cash transcended musical boundaries, borrowing inspiration from country music and from the likes of Woody Guthrie, Bob Dylan, Bruce Springsteen, and other major American artists.

Cash's creative juices weren't just found in music. She turned to writing, where the same kind of candid look at life gave her books an irresistible vitality. Short stories, children's stories, and a memoir enabled Rosanne Cash to make her mark in contemporary American prose. Today, she continues to write, record, and perform. Her album *The River and the Thread* (2014) is a critically acclaimed musical travelog through America.

> "Those old studios were fantastic — Woodland Studio in Nashville, where those great country songs were recorded. Amazing. The Quonset Hut in Nashville, the Record Plant in New York, Electric Lady. Some of those great old studios, you know, you go in and you just get some kinda vibe. You gotta wonder what kind of thing was raining down from heaven on Memphis at that time."

ON RECORDING STUDIOS

I've been in the business a really long time, and I've seen the recording process change so much from when it was the norm to go to a mastering lab and cut straight into the mother vinyl and press from there, to where everything is digital.

When I was a kid, there was an almost mythic power to recording consoles. They kinda scared me. They were as big as a spaceship, and I didn't understand all these different channels and these knobs and different lights, the patch bay with all of these cords coming out of them. What did it all mean? It wasn't just furniture to me. It had its own imbued power. And as I grew to understand it, it still didn't lose any of its thrill. Sitting at a console—it's so exciting!

At the time [in the early fifties] it was a vortex. You had Sun Records, and you had Jerry Lee Lewis and my dad and Carl Perkins and Roy Orbison and Elvis recording at Sun right at that time. You would think that Sun Records was a grand structure, because of how large it looms in music history. But it's just a small room.

Those old studios were fantastic—Woodland Studio in Nashville, where those great country songs were recorded. Amazing. The Quonset Hut in Nashville, the Record Plant in New York, Electric Lady. Some of those great old studios, you know, you go in and you just get some kinda vibe. You gotta wonder what kind of thing was raining down from heaven on Memphis at that time.

Each studio had its own personality. I feel that way about studios. Going to the old Columbia studios with my dad, sitting at that board, you know, feeling the history that happened there—my dad and Bob Dylan in that room recording *Nashville Skyline.* That's heavy.

My father was so comfortable in studios, and he never walked in insecure about it.

He'd spend as much time in studios as he did in his car or anywhere else. That was his natural habitat. Like an animal in the wild, that was his habitat.

I was just in the old Capitol building in Los Angeles, and we went in that room where Frank Sinatra recorded with Nelson Riddle—those great classic records, and that microphone, you know? It was just goose bumpy. There are ghosts there, my friend.

ON THE ARTIST–PRODUCER RELATIONSHIP

There's a range of production styles among producers from being totally hands-on, to producers who are more like executive producers who come and check in once in a while but let other people do the other work. There are producer-arrangers who actually arrange songs, and there are producers who might even arrange and record. I've worked with all kinds, but I prefer working with someone in a really intense experience, where it's a real collaboration.

The producer-artist relationship is something that took me a while to understand. I mean, as a kid, it was a very vague concept. You know, you heard a record, and you thought they made that record and somebody must have recorded it. But you didn't realize that there was somebody functioning in a director capacity for an album. And, of course, as I started my own career and saw the importance of that relationship and how much I depended on a producer, it was an eye-opener.

Johnny Cash, 1990

I produced one record myself, and I had to pare it down to understand my own limitations, that there were certain voicings I didn't hear or didn't know how to articulate. So now I am so comfortable with the producer relationship and so happy to have someone who knows what I don't know. He uses what I know and I use what he knows and it's great. I mean, I have no interest in producing my own records anymore. There's nothing I need to prove there.

ON JOHNNY CASH

When he was a kid, he wanted to be a singer. They could not afford singing lessons, but his mom took jobs to make extra money so that my dad could have singing lessons. By the second lesson, the singing teacher brought him home and said to my grandmother, "This boy has got something special, and I don't wanna mess it up. So don't bring him back."

My dad's voice was roughhewn. It had some cotton fields in it. The stark honesty of his voice—no flourishes, no artifice or falsity to it. He didn't do gymnastics with his voice. Wasn't a showoff. He just delivered the story in the most honest way, the most authentic. I think that's why people responded. People respond to authenticity because there's some kind of chemical vibration that comes out when you're being real. And they recognized that in my dad.

❧ sheila e. ❧

Don't ever say the drums or percussion are instruments meant to be played by men. First off, you'd be dead wrong. Second, you'd probably arouse the wrath of Sheila Escovedo, better known as Sheila E. That's because Sheila E. is a first-class drummer and percussionist. Male drummers respect her; some even see her as an important influence, as does just about any female today who sits behind a kit or picks up a pair of sticks. Fact is, Sheila E. eliminates gender bias in the world of drums. The way she likes to tell it, there are only good drummers and not-so-good drummers. Sheila E. is certainly the former.

Sheila also has what other musicians crave, and either they have it, or they don't: good genes, a lineage that organically links them to their instrument. The Escovedo family, some say, was born into music. Sheila's father, Pete, played percussion with Carlos Santana, back when the band and the man were introducing mainstream rock to the richly percussive sounds of Latino rock and blues. Her brothers are percussionists, and her uncle is Alejandro Escovedo, the noted Americana singer-songwriter. Tito Puente was her godfather.

Sheila began her career playing in her father's post-Santana band, Azteca. Her playing was such that she attracted the attention of artists such as Billy Cobham, Herbie Han-

cock, Marvin Gaye, Diana Ross, and George Duke, all of whom either had Sheila E. play in their touring bands, or on their albums, or both. It was when she was with Duke that Sheila met Prince, who promptly took her under his wing. It was Prince who insisted she become a solo artist. Sheila E.'s debut album, *The Glamorous Life,* was released in 1984 at the height of Prince's invasion of funk-rock. *The Glamorous Life* was Sheila E.'s calling card, proof that a female percussionist could become a pop star as well as an in-demand session and touring player—and make them all work. And to be certain no one missed it, in 1987 Prince featured Sheila in his band after she started as the opening act of his Purple Rain Tour (1984–85).

What has made Sheila E.'s work truly shine is the way she carefully balances funk, pop, rock, and Latin music in her playing. Her rhythms have sass, her solos sink their teeth into the percussive traditions celebrated by Puente and her father. Yet she can be pop perfect in her fills and beats, making her not just versatile, but able to fluently speak a half dozen or so rhythm languages.

Sheila E. continues to perform as a solo artist and works with other artists as a session player and on tour, and she tours with her own band as well.

ON HEARING
EARLY RHYTHMS

For me it all started with listening to my dad play music every single day. The tables and chairs were really congas and timbales, bongos, hand percussion, maracas, guiras, shakers. The house was filled with "toys," and I remember listening to artists like Tito Puente, Mongo Santamaria, Miles Davis, Eddie Palmieri. My dad had an incredible list of artists and LPs that he listened to.

My dad played, my uncles played—they came over and played, so it was my dad and his brother playing percussion and then my other uncle also played bass. And then my other younger uncles played guitar. They would have jam sessions in the house. Sometimes there wouldn't even be any electrical instruments, it would just be all percussion—congas, timbales, bongos, hand toys. It was loud! People knew that we lived on that block. Some days we'd wake up in the morning to go to school and we would see people we didn't know laying on the floor in the living room 'cuz they were hanging out all night playing. It was a lot of fun!

So being brought up in a household that had music every single day was pretty amazing—it was the norm for us.

ON LATIN JAZZ
INFLUENCES

Latin jazz consisted of timbales, congas, a little bit of bongos, and some drums. And we were able to play percussively around each other, and not have to obey the clave [a five-stroke rhythmic pattern used in Afro-Cuban music]. For our Latin jazz music we didn't apply that clave to what we played. On the East Coast they stuck by that clave and their parts that they played, and

they weren't really allowed, in that music, to steer away from it. But on the West Coast we were allowed to play around those rhythms, so we were a little bit more free.

Things started changing when disco came out. A lot of the drummers were afraid that they would lose a gig because of the drum machines, but then they added a lot of percussion to those songs, and the dance then became kinda like Latin.

Salsa dancing and dancing Latin—we all used to talk about how it made us feel. It's a lifestyle. It's what we love to do. When you hear rhythms, you automatically wanna dance. When they started adding percussion instruments to disco I thought it was kinda cool to add those elements of the Latin percussion in pop and disco music, and it made me want to dance.

When Marvin Gaye came out with "What's Going On," that conga drum—that rhythm—is something that every percussionist was excited about, because that was a Latin instrument—a percussive instrument—that was in an R&B song that everyone knew. If you were a percussion player, everyone would say, "Hey, do you know that Marvin Gaye rhythm—that *doon-doonkadoodoonkadoonka?*" It's something that came from the Latin community and was simplified to fit R&B music.

Carlos Santana really brought in something totally different that none of us had experienced or heard before. It was a big deal, it was like, Wow—this guy is playing rock guitar, in a sense, with drums, timbales, congas, bongos, and then all of the singers were playing hand percussion as well. It was something that changed music. It was a sound that no one had heard. And for us in the Bay Area [of San Francisco] it

OPPOSITE
Sheila E. performing in 2014

Sheila E., 1980

was a big deal, because it was something we were proud of, first of all, and it was something that us as Latin people could relate to, because those percussion instruments that were traditionally used for salsa music were now being used in rock. And the way that he utilized that was awesome. The Latin community was very, very proud of seeing those instruments that we love so much in the mainstream. It was crossing over, and now everyone heard it—not just the Latin community but everyone else. Carlos Santana did that for all of us.

When we talk about American popular music, I think Latin influences sometimes get buried. Right now, Latin music—Latin people—are acknowledged

more than they've ever been. It's been a long time coming.

ON STUDIO DRUMMING

When I'm playing live, if I take a drum solo, I'm not gonna say to the audience, "Excuse me! Hold on! I just messed this up; let's do it again." We never do that. So why would I do that in the studio? In that situation, I want to play the song in one take and just play it the way it feels right. By the time you start editing what you just played, the soul and spirit of that part is gone. And you don't feel it anymore. So for me, as a live artist, I love recording in an element of it being live.

I embraced the drum machine because it was something new. I love technology, I

Performing with Prince, 2007

loved that something in this machine was doing something different. Having that machine and the freedom to use it differently than anyone else allowed me to develop my own sound. I love using old and new. So the drum machine was new, percussion was old, but old and new together was what made my sound.

ON WORKING WITH PRINCE

Working with Prince in the studio was a little bit different than any other artist that I had recorded with. He wouldn't spend the time to get a drum sound or percussion congas, whatever. They'd put the mics up, and they'd say, "Ready?" And we'd just start recording. There was no "getting any sound." It's what it was. To me, that's what makes his sound. It's all the nastiness that's happening with everybody's instrument—the bass players buzzing and leaving it funky like that. And so not cleaning up the stuff actually makes this part of his sound. Him just playing it, recording the way that it is. I just think that this is a time when people are spending way too much studio time getting drum sounds.

What I love is the human feel. Even with technology, I think that at the end of the day what we all look for in a record is the artist.

❧ darryl mcdaniels ❧

Hip-hop has had a remarkable run. A music form born in Bronx basements in the early 1970s, rap, as it was first called, unlike virtually all popular music prior to it, relied much more on rhythm and beats than on melody. It was minus the standard instruments, namely the electric guitar, which America had so routinely relied on in popular music for nearly a century, and instead used the turntable as one of the main ways to make music that was essential to its growing legion of fans.

From the beginning, hip-hop embraced words—words that rhymed and were used for boasting, and, later on, for expressing outrage. Words became its soul food, its source of nourishment, and they nestled up nicely to the beats and rhythms that filled out a hip-hop track. But before hip-hop turned angry and before it shoved aside rock and roll and stood fully in the pop spotlight, in effect becoming America's pop music, hip-hop stood at a crossroads. The group that propelled it forward was Run-D.M.C.

The group consisted of Joey Simmons, aka DJ Run; Jason Mizell, aka Jam Master Jay; and Darryl McDaniels, aka D.M.C. The trio grew up in Queens listening to the early hip-hop sounds of Grandmaster Flash, the Sugarhill Gang, Kurtis Blow, and other pioneers. In 1981, Run-D.M.C. was born and the group hit the ground running. Its debut single, "It's Like That," was a major hit on black radio. The follow-up "Hard Times" did equally well. Both singles featured the trademark Run-D.M.C. sound: large vocals, fat bottoms, and, most interestingly, a surprising connection to rock, something not usually found in earlier hip-hop singles.

Run-D.M.C. wasn't afraid to boast about its rock connection, either. Other top tracks from Run-D.M.C. included "Rock Box," "King of Rock," and "Can You Rock It Like This." As a result, Run-D.M.C. was the perfect hip-hop group to bring in the increasingly intrigued hip white audience, which didn't understand exactly what was going on in hip-hop, but wanted to learn.

In 1986 Run-D.M.C. released *Raising Hell,* one of the most important albums of the decade and the first rap album nominated for a Grammy. It was the work that truly connected hip-hop and rock. Darryl McDaniels, the group's guiding force and main rapper, had sensed the bond coming on, and was ready when producer Rick Rubin suggested that Run-D.M.C. do a video of their version of "Walk This Way," and that they do it with Aerosmith, the band that had created the hard-rock classic. The video was a smash; it broke down the barriers between rock and hip-hop and in the process made Run-D.M.C. major stars. Not surprisingly, the video also re-ignited Aerosmith's artistic energy and career. The video had a lot to do with Run-D.M.C. being inducted into the Rock and Roll Hall of Fame in 2009.

The influence of McDaniels and Run-D.M.C. wasn't all about music. The style—the bling, the untied Adidas sneakers, the baggy pants—that came to define hip-hop pretty much started with Run-D.M.C. They could rap and they could rock, they could style and they could command attention. Darryl McDaniels and Run-D.M.C. could do it all—and did.

ON RADIO

The first music I heard growing up was on a radio station in New York. They used to play Jim Croce, Harry Chapin, the Beatles, Elton John. But they also played James Brown, Sly and the Family Stone.

Everybody was into soul power and James Brown and the Jackson Five and bell-bottoms and high heels, but for some reason, the music that really grabbed me was rock and roll, and it was those rock groups—Led Zeppelin, Dylan, the Beatles, the Stones—that impacted me. And the great thing about the radio was that they played all this great music.

Radio changed a lot since then; radio now is so programmed. It's like when I hear the words *program director,* I always tell the listener, you'd better watch out. Today you hear the same twelve songs over and over. Back then, you were exposed to different sounds, different concepts, different ideas. You would never know what you were going to hear when you turned the radio on. You'd hear Janis Joplin's voice wailing and right after that you would hear James Brown and then you would hear Marvin Gaye, and then it would veer off and you would hear George Harrison with some Indian music, sitars and stuff in it. So back then, you were exposed to a whole realm of music where there were no expectations and there was emotions and there was no direction.

Nowadays, kids are missing a great life experience. Kids today only experience what is being given to them. Whether it's

through these music channels or radio, everything is so programmed. They're receiving the same thing over and over.

Also, kids don't have the experience of going to the record store and walking in those doors to get your record. I used to take my allowance and go get this record. The record store was a world where you would get the record you came to get, but then you would hear this other song that was playing and you would go, "Oh, my God, what's that?"

Kids today don't get that experience. They don't look at music from an artistic standpoint or a creative standpoint. But more importantly, they don't look at it as a life-impacting event.

ON THE MUSIC OF THE SIXTIES

In the sixties, those musicians—Bob Dylan, John Lennon, John Fogerty—didn't care what people thought about what they were singing. If there was something to say about civil rights, they sang a song about it. From all sides. If they had something to say about the Vietnam War, they sang a song about it. From all sides. The artists of the day don't address the issues. The music of today is not the voice of the people anymore.

But Fogarty was the voice, John Lennon was the voice, Bob Dylan was the voice. Even though Marvin Gaye started out sexy, he did "What's Going On." James Brown, you know, soul brother, soul power and all

Run-DMC in 1986. *From Left*: DMC (Darryl McDaniels), DJ Run (Joseph Simmons), and Jam Master Jay (Jason William Mizell).

of this, he did political, socially conscious records. They were our voices. They spoke what needed to be said and what needed to be heard because they recorded their music as we lived our lives. And people didn't have to agree with you. The beautiful thing about it was that it was our truth. Whether you were black, white, Puerto Rican, young, old, whether you was Ku Klux Klan, Protestant, it addressed all the issues that we lived in.

Those artists were our lives, and our lives were on those records.

ON HIP-HOP CULTURE
AND RAP MUSIC

When I do my lectures, I explain that hip-hop represents the total existence of the artist. It's what rock and roll was and what music is supposed to be. The way we dress is the fashion of the hip-hop culture. The way we dance is the dance of the hip-hip culture, and the way we draw and do graffiti, take pictures, is the art of the hip-hop culture. So hip-hop itself is the culture.

When you look at so-called gangsta rap or when you look at the thug image in hip-hop, these rappers say, I'm just telling stories about where I come from. And I'll look at that and say, Yeah, but you're not giving a complete picture. Because even in the dirt-poor ghetto, everybody isn't a drug dealer, a pimp, or prostitute. What about the story of the hard-working lady that raised six kids, sent them all to college, none of them went to jail, none of those girls are bitches and ho's, and none of them are thugs and selling it? You need to sing about that, too. So that a kid in Memphis, Tennessee, can know that in this world, there's information, education, motivation, inspiration.

Hip-hop was a reaction to Reaganomics. Hip-hop caught fire because there was a cultural rebellious turning point, because these young individuals who were oppressed had to do something to be heard and get people's attention. So we turned up that raw guitar, we took our music to the parks, took other people's music, made some noise, and raised some hell.

I mean, it was crazy back then. There was poverty, crime, gangs, drugs, the education system was really bad. We had nothing. And what we did was we sang about those issues. Broken glass everywhere, life being hard in the ghetto, crime, drugs. We sang about everything that was really bad because we wanted to get it off our chests. But once we put all those issues and that information out there, we also looked at what we were singing about and we also sang about solutions. We started writing, performing, demonstrating, presenting music that was full of hope.

When you look at Native Americans and their drums, their beats, their music, it wasn't about their politics. It wasn't even about their religion. It was about their entire existence. It was about the music; it was about the beat being the heartbeat of their existence. Everything, the emotions, their feelings. They played a beat before they would go to battle. They played a beat when they would have a marriage. They played a beat when they had a celebration. They played a beat when the kid was growing up. They played a beat when they went out and had a successful hunt.

Today we still play music at the wedding, when we graduate, when we have parties and all of that. And you know

"Hip-hop caught fire because there was a cultural rebellious turning point, because these young individuals who were oppressed had to do something to be heard and get people's attention. So we turned up that raw guitar, we took our music to the parks, took other people's music, made some noise, and raised some hell."

what's crazy? That the whole spiritual, physical, and emotional relationship to our music has been forgotten now. Music was once the pulse and center of our lives, of our expressions, of our emotions, of our issues, and of our conditions.

ON THE POWER OF MUSIC

Music is a universal language. It succeeds where politics and religions fail. It's timeless. There are no barriers in music. The only barriers are in our hearts and minds.

The power of music to effect change has been demonstrated all throughout history.

When rock and roll came along, the musicians became the real voice of the people. What you couldn't get in the newspaper, what you couldn't get from the media, you would get from the music. That's what hip-hop was. Hip-hop is us taking a stand to be heard truthfully, and addressing the issues and conditions and circumstances that need to be addressed that might not be addressed in the media. As Chuck D said, hip-hop was the CNN of the streets.

That's why recorded music is the best way to teach history. It's a wonderful tool to educate. It's a great medium to inspire, motivate, to share knowledge. It's about purpose and destiny. Never let your situation define who you are. And if you need some releases, there's always that song, that piano, that verse, that voice, that beat, that cut, that scratch, that guitar riff that's going to save your life.

PHOTOGRAPHY CREDITS

Photographs by Robert Essel

2, 5, 12, 15, 19, 23, 24, 26, 29, 32, 37, 43, 46, 47, 48, 50, 53, 55, 56, 61, 66, 70, 76, 78, 79, 81, 82, 83, 84, 94, 98, 107, 108, 112, 117, 124, 128

Photographs from the Beatles Book Photo Library

Pages 9, 10, 11, 45, 52

Photographs from Getty Images

Page 4: Imagno; page 7: GAB Archive; page 16: Michael Ochs Archives; page 17: Capital Records; page 20: Elliot Landy; page 21: John Cohen; page 28: Don Hunstein © Sony Music Entertainment; page 30: GAB Archive; page 31: Kevin Mazur; page 34 (top): Michael Ochs Archives; page 34 (bottom): GAB Archive; page 35 (top): Kai Shuman; page 35 (bottom): Robert Kelley; page 38: Michael Ochs Archives; page 40: Joan Adlen Photography; page 41: Giles Petard; page 44: Ethan Miller; page 54: C. Flanigan; page 58: Kirk West; page 59: Jeremy Fletcher; page 62: Robert Knight Archive; page 63: Rob Verhorst; page 64: Jack Robinson; page 68 (top): Hiroyuki Ito; page 68 (bottom): Hiroyuki Ito; page 69: Hiroyuki Ito; page 72: Michael Ochs Archives; page 74: Brian Rasic; page 75: Kevin Mazur; page 80: Terry O'Neill; page 86: Michael Putland; page 87: Ullstein Bild; page 97: Frans Schellekens; page 99: Kevin Winter; page 102: Michael Putland; page 103: Paul R. Giunta; page 104: Richard E. Aaron; page 105: Peter Still; page 109: CBS Photo Archive; page 110: Richard E. Aaron/Referns; page 115: Robert Knight Archive; page 116: GAB Archive; page 119: Debra L. Rothenberg; page 121: David A. Walega; page 122: Michael Ochs Archives; page 123: Kevin Winter; page 127: Ebet Roberts

Additional Credits

Page 73: © John Craig Oxman, all rights reserved, photos by John Peden; page 88: Fabio Lovino; page 90: Fabio Lovino; page 91: Fabio Lovino; page 92: Henrik Nansen; page 100: Sam Jones/ Trunk Archive